The Wakefield Mysteries

'Adrian Henri's version, commissioned specially as the grand finale of the Wakefield 100 Festival, is a triumph of breaking down the language barrier yet keeping the true spirit and vitality of the plays intact, highlighting the imagery and parallels and giving the words a new poetry, which looks set to make the script a popular modern classic.'
(Amanda Marsh, *Yorkshire Evening Post*)

'Henri has gone for the heart and gut of the original bawdy, satirical Middle English . . . , dismantling it to create a new, popular poetry, catching natural speech rhythms, dialect, song and rhyme to tell a truth that's both earthy and celebratory, and sings clear as a bell. . . . Affectionately, Henri has woven rich folk mythology into a glorious school play . . . its text should be grabbed by all enlightened drama teachers.'
(Norma Cohen, *Times Educational Supplement*)

Adrian Henri was born in Birkenhead in 1932 and lives in Liverpool. He is a poet, painter, playwright, songwriter and occasional art critic and regularly exhibits paintings. His publications include: *Collected Poems* (1986), *Wish You Were Here* (1990), *The Phantom Lollipop Lady* and *Rhinestone Rhino* (poems for children, 1986 and 1989), *Eric the Punk Cat* and *The Postman's Palace* (1933 and 1990), and *Box* (poems for teenagers, 1990). His plays include: *I Want* (with Nell Dunn, 1986), *The Husband, the Wife and the Stranger* (BBC TV, 1986) and (with others) *Fears and Miseries of the Third Term* (1989).

Methuen's Theatre Classics

Büchner
Danton's Death
(English version by Howard Brenton)
Woyzeck
(translated by John McKendrick;
introduced by Michael Patterson)

Chekhov
The Cherry Orchard
Three Sisters
The Seagull
Uncle Vanya
(translated and introduced by Michael Frayn)
The Sneeze
Wild Honey
(translated, adapted and introduced by Michael Frayn)

Euripides
The Bacchae
(English version by Wole Soyinka)

Jarry
The Ubu Plays
(translated by Cyril Connolly and Simon Watson Taylor;
edited with an introduction by Simon Watson Taylor)

Synge
The Playboy of the Western World
(introduced by T. R. Henn)

Wedekind
Spring Awakening
(translated by Edward Bond;
introduced by Edward and Elisabeth Bond)

Wilde
The Importance of Being Earnest
(introduced by Adeline Hartcup)

The Wakefield Mysteries

adapted by Adrian Henri

Methuen Drama

A METHUEN THEATRE CLASSIC

First published in this adaptation as a paperback original by Methuen Drama, Michelin House, 81 Fulham Road, London SW3 6RB and distributed in the United States of America by HEB Inc., 361 Hanover Street, Portsmouth, New Hampshire NH 03801 3959.

The Wakefield Mysteries adaptation copyright © 1988, 1991 Adrian Henri *Introduction* copyright © 1991 Adrian Henri

The author has asserted his moral rights.

ISBN 0-413-66210-1

A CIP catalogue record for this book is available from the British Library.

The front cover shows a detail from the sixteenth-century picture *Passion de Valenciennes* by Hubert Cailleau, reproduced by kind permission of the Bibliothèque Nationale, Paris.

The photograph on the back cover shows Adrian Henri with Joe McAleese (God), left, and Mick Martin (Lucifer), right. The photograph is by Don McPhee and is copyright © The Guardian Newspaper.

The map of Pontefract Castle on p xi is reproduced courtesy of Wakefield MDC, Museums, Galleries and Castles

Printed and bound in Great Britain by Cox & Wyman Ltd, Cardiff Road, Reading

Introduction

I began work on the Wakefield Mysteries by visiting the site – the ruins of Pontefract Castle in Yorkshire – with the Director, Graham Devlin, and working out roughly what would happen where, and then sitting down with him and deciding on the basic shape and order of the work: the original, episodic piece, lasting some sixteen hours, had to be reduced to two modern-length plays (each roughly an hour and a half), each with an interval. Where would the natural breaks be? What technical problems might affect them? Much of the early work on the script was done in collaboration with Graham, and cuts, additions, and rewrites went on almost until the opening.

The original production was a 'promenade' one, and specific to the site, with the plays done on alternate weekday evenings, and end-to-end at weekends. The plays are, however, performable in any large space, indoor or out, separate or together, and the stage directions adapted accordingly, though the principle of certain areas having particular associations – Eden/The Baptism, the 'Baddies' (Pharaoh, Herod, Pilate) – should be kept to as much as possible. Similarly, though I wrote the plays for a very large cast, the numbers could be varied considerably by 'doubling' where necessary.

I think it is important to note how much repetition is used, how one situation echoes an earlier one: I used the song 'Father, Father . . .' to mark three key episodes of father/son betrayal; the Wakefield Master's gloriously irreverent idea of Mack's wife passing off the stolen lamb as a newborn child is a deliberate pre-parody of the Nativity tableau, and should be seen to be so. The setting and costumes that Devlin and designer Marise Rose devised were based on the concept of a rural, farming community, appropriate to both the Jewish tribe and the Yorkshire shepherds of the original.

As a Liverpudlian I deliberately avoided trying to write 'Yorkshire'; however, I have used some general Northern idioms, and some of the rhyme-words demand typically flat Northern vowels – 'command'/'hand', for example, caused one actor problems. What is important is to keep the feeling that these were workers, artisans, farmers from one community playing the biblical parts. I don't feel anything crucial has been left out of the original plays; there was much repetition and 'the story so far' because each playlet was performed by a different trade-guild in a different part of the town. In a multi-cultural society it was necessary to suppress the gratuitous anti-Muslim rhetoric – Mohammed gets almost as bad a press as the Devil – the Crusades obviously being an important issue; similarly, the anti-woman bias of the theology of the time has been altered slightly without, I hope, taking the edge away from the original text. This is in no way an academic transcription, but an attempt to preserve the spirit of the medieval texts in an actable modern version.

Replacing the team of horses in the Cain/Abel episode with a tractor is a joke that needn't necessarily be repeated: some form of pantomime horse routine could be used. We decided to make Garcio a girl, despite the name, for no good reason except to provide a good, comic female part. A male actor could do the part with suitable dialogue changes [as provided on pp. 97–100 of this book].

We know that hymns and carols were interpolated in Mystery plays, which themselves grew out of dramatised elements of church ritual, so my idea of adding songs at moments of tension is, I hope, justified. The *Magnificat* and *Stabat Mater* are adapted from orthodox Christian texts, 'Go Down Moses' is a well-known spiritual, and the plain-chant *Dies Irae* is the most chilling (and most quoted) piece of music I know. Most of Andy Roberts's music was recorded electronically, but sung live.

We live in a secular society in which religion no longer plays the all-embracing role it did in the Middle Ages; I hope, nevertheless, that the power, the drama and the humour of these familiar stories will be as relevant to present-day audiences. What the plays are about, for me, is above all man and woman's struggle to choose between dark and light, envy and humility, pride and compassion.

Adrian Henri
May 1991

This adaptation of *The Wakefield Mysteries* was first performed at Pontefract Castle as part of the Wakefield centenary celebrations in July 1988, with the following cast (in order of appearance):

Part One

GOD	Joe McAleese	
ANGEL (*speaking*)	Jo Patt	
LUCIFER/SATAN	Mick Martin	
GABRIEL	Liz Heywood	
GOOD ANGELS	Fiona Edwards	Della Appleyard
BAD ANGELS	Bevil Edwards	Kevin Shipley
	Lisa Baker	Gloria Lang
ADAM	Richard Betts	
EVE	Vicky Higgins	
GARCIO	Rachel Phelps	
CAIN	Jeremy Walker	
ABEL	Nick Ledgard	
NOAH	Tim Eagle	
MRS NOAH (UXOR)	Liz Heywood	
NOAH'S CHILDREN	Darren Chambers	Libby Fell
	Rachel Woodhouse	Jonathan Wadey
	Anthony Foster	Sarah Butterworth
ANIMALS	Louise Smith	Lisa Baker
	Louise Booth	Andrew Howard
	Steven Casey	Jason Rayne
	Vicky Iveson	Alice Shaw
	Donna Green	Karen Agnew
	Penny Layden	Michaela Sayers
	Mark Barnes	Debbie Hopkins
	Stuart Walton	Stephen Nunn
	Valerie Agnew	Kevin Shipley
	Heather Brown	Martin Moizer
	Claire Frost	Steven Keighley
	Jade Langley	Jeffrey Smith

MUSICIANS	George Faux *(fiddle)* Amanda Berry *(flute)*	Rachel Moss *(clarinet)* Amanda Brook *(clarinet)*
ABRAHAM	Graham D'Albert	
ISAAC	Thomas Cook	
SOPRANO VOICE	Andrew Bryant Jonathan Graves	Richard Whitham
MOSES	Mick Scott	
ISRAELITES/RED SEA	Jeremy Walker Neil Shand Judith Carlyle Eleanor Mullis Kylie Robinson Vicky Higgins Jonathan Wadey Darren Chambers Gary Whittaker Anthony Foster Abi Briant Brenda Smith Jane Tuska Sarah Butterworth	Lisa Baker Liz Heywood Jeffrey Smith Craig Smith Eleanor Dearle Della Appleyard Reg Lavine Nicola Willoughby Gloria Lang Penny Layden Thomas Cook Michael Dargon Jonathan Lazenby
BANNER DANCERS	Lindy Rowley Rachel Woodhouse Abi Briant	Georgina Gallivan Chris Walsham Charlotte Ripley
PHARAOH	Austin Allen	
CAPTAIN	Neil Shand	
PHARAOH'S COURT	Kevin Shipley Libby Fell Rachel Phelps Roger Green Carl Rozenbroek Gary Whittaker Bevil Edwards	Tim Eagle Neil Shand June Cooper Richard Betts Peter Ayre Laurence Rayner
MARY	Penny Layden	
JOSEPH	George Broadhead	

KINGS	Gloria Lang	Libby Fell
	Neil Shand	
KING'S SERVANTS	Jane Tuska	Della Appleyard
	Sarah Butterworth	Abi Briant
HEROD	Peter Ayre	
HEROD'S MINISTERS	Alberta Burns	Roger Green
	Eleanor Mullis	
SHEPHERDS	Darren Chambers	Eleanor Dearle
	Brenda Smith	
MACK	Keven Shipley	
GILL	Liz Butler	

Part Two
(as Part One) plus:

MOTHERS	Rachel Phelps	Helen Lindley
	Jane Tuska	Mary Wilson
	Brenda Smith	
SOLDIERS	Thomas Spencer	Paul Bowen
	Richard Betts	
MOTHERS' CHORUS	Kylie Robinson	Sarah Oldknow
	Judith Carlyle	Eleanor Dearle
	Lorraine Wadsworth	Eleanor Mullis
	Penny Layden	
JOHN THE BAPTIST	Kevin Shipley	
JESUS	Nick Ledgard	
PONTIUS PILATE	Austin Allen	
ANNAS	Roger Green	
CAIAPHAS	Liz Butler	
LAZARUS	Laurence Rayner	
JUDAS	Richard Betts	
PETER	Ken Hawlor	
MARY MAGDALENE	Judith Carlyle	
MARTHA	Lorraine Wadsworth	

DISCIPLES	Paul Bowen	George Faux
	George Broadhead	Carl Rozenbroek
	Jonathan Wadey	Reg Lavine
	Francis Duncan	John Holmes
	Craig Smith	Thomas Spencer
PILATE'S SOLDIERS	Gary Whittaker	Neil Shand
	Craig Smith	
TORTURERS	Peter Ayre	Jeremy Walker
SIMON OF CYRENE	Laurence Rayner	
DEVILS	Helen Lindley	Sarah Waring
	Anthony Foster	
BAND	Sheepscar Interchange	

All other roles played by members of the company.

Directed by Graham Devlin
Assistant Directors Gill Wright (choreography)
                     Al Dix
                     Tony Lidington
                     Simon Lanzon
Designed by Marise Rose
Composer and Musical Director Andy Roberts
Assistant Musical Director John Megginson
Lighting Designer Steve Whitson
Production Manager Edward De Pledge

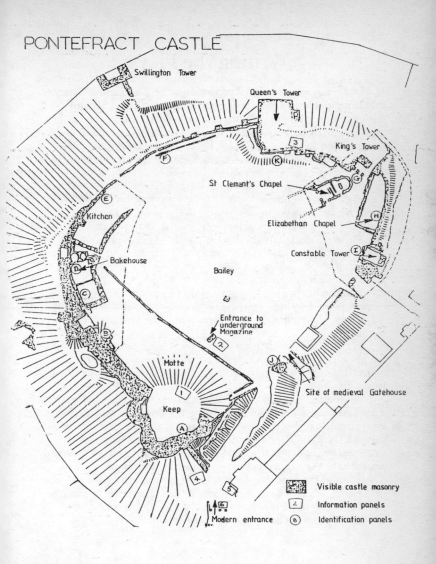

PONTEFRACT CASTLE

Swillington Tower

Queen's Tower

King's Tower

St Clement's Chapel

Elizabethan Chapel

Constable Tower

Kitchen

Bakehouse

Bailey

Entrance to
underground
Magazine

Motte

Keep

Site of medieval Gatehouse

Modern entrance

Visible castle masonry

Information panels

Identification panels

Writing the Plays

My first reaction to being asked to adapt the Wakefield Mystery cycle into modern English was excitement, challenge. Second thoughts were more apprehensive: thirty-two rhymed playlets in medieval English, five of which are, by common consent, amongst the finest works in the language. These five are by the unknown genius we know only as the Wakefield Master, who covered a huge range from the sheerest bawdy to the exalted devotional in a complex verse-form of his own devising. Eventually I decided that the original rhymeschemes would sound too mechanical today; I wrote the plays as poems for voices, in the idiom I'd write in normally: formal devices played off against natural speech-rhythms.

I also decided early on that, at points of heightened drama, I'd use songs rather than dialogue, and that local music-making was an important resource: Andy Roberts, the composer and Musical Director, is a longtime collaborator and friend.

I've tried to avoid archaisms of the 'Thee' and 'O'er' variety. Contrariwise, I wanted to avoid obvious anachronisms (Herod's soldiers as SAS men, say), and try to retain the timeless feel of the original.

Having been brought up on the 1611 King James Bible, I had the ghastly example of the New English Bible – the literary equivalent of polystyrene junk food – as a solemn warning of what might go wrong.

The more I worked on the Wakefield version of the familiar stories, the more I realised how strong the dramatic structure was, how parallels and echoes (Abraham and Isaac/The Crucifixion) run through the plays. I've cut a deal of wearisome recapitulation necessary to the original staging, and the sequence has been slightly re-cast to fit the site, and the staging as two autonomous plays. There is nothing here that I don't feel is sanctioned by the original – Mrs Noah, Mack the sheepstealer and the other extra-Biblical characters are all there – and I hope I've captured some of the vitality, exuberance and passion of the original cycle.

Adrian Henri
July 1988

Part One

Creation to Nativity

Music. GOD *processes to throne with* ANGEL. *The full company take up positions on the Keep. As the song finishes, all withdraw, leaving* GOD, ANGELS, LUCIFER.

CHORUS.
> *Greed and Disobedience*
> *Envy, Pride and Sin*
> *A never changing pattern*
> *See another piece begin*

> Lucifer the bright angel
> Committed the sin of pride
> Cast like a leper from heaven
> With nowhere left to hide   (*Chorus.*)

> Adam and Eve in the garden
> Tasted forbidden fruit
> Now they are banned for ever
> Naked and destitute   (*Chorus.*)

> Cain was jealous of Abel
> Slew him on the dark hill
> Committed the world's first murder
> The killing continues still   (*Chorus.*)

> Herod was told of Jesus
> The child who will rule alone
> He murdered all the small children
> To preserve his earthly throne   (*Chorus.*)

> Christ was betrayed by Judas
> And they nailed Him to the cross
> Last piece of the tragic pattern
> Emblem of all our loss   (*Chorus.*)

> *During* GOD's *speech sunrays are unrolled down the Keep and raised on a frame behind the throne.*

GOD.
> I am the world. In the beginning
> was the word. I am the beginning.
> And the word was the world
> and all things in it.

Maker of Heaven and Earth,
Alpha and Omega.

I gave the word, and divided night
from day. The heavens do as I say
and all the stars spring to my command.
Let there be light, I say.
This I do on the first day.

At a touch of my hand the waters part,
I bring forth the land.
Mountains and rivers, lakes and valleys
leap to do my bidding.
This I do on the second day.

Like clothing for the bare, shivering planet
I conjure trees, grass, fruit and flowers.
Great prairies, shady bowers
all bring forth seed in abundance.
This I do on the third day.

I caused the sun to shine by day,
I caused the moon to shine by night.
Like winding a clock
I set the seasons in their courses.
This I did on the fourth day.

I peopled the air with birds, the condor
and the tiny linnet. Great whales
and little sprats frolicked in the waters.
The seas and skies were filled with my handiwork.
This I did on the fifth day.

And I saw that my work was good:
pleased with my work I filled it with
creatures great and small,
hot- or cold-blooded, walking or creeping.
All this I did on the sixth day.

Alpha and Omega,
Maker of Heaven and Earth.

ANGEL.
Maker of Earth and Heaven,
the seas and skies and the seven stars,
we sing Your praise.
In these six days

You have done such wonders
as none of us can understand,
the power of Your hand
divides the land.
The sun by day, the moon by night
to give us light. But none so bright
as he that is brightest among us,
Lucifer, *Luce Ferens*,
the very carrier of light.
Surely, Lord of the Holy Trinity,
none shines more brightly than he?

GOD *has exited by now.* LUCIFER *comes forward, sings.*

LUCIFER.
I am Lucifer, Prince of light,
my face eclipses the night.
Brightest of all
in Heaven.

So beautiful, so bright,
none can resist the sight.
All that see
worship me

Why should they not? Why just He?
Surely this Lord of Trinity
Is not alone
fit for a throne?

Now I'll come into my own. Let's see
How well this mighty seat,
this noble throne
fits me.

He sits on GOD's *throne, preens himself.*

Now then, brothers and sisters,
Doesn't it suit me just as well?
Doesn't this seat of mine
look fine?

1ST BAD ANGEL.
Yes, I must admit it suits you,
you look the part without a doubt.

1ST GOOD ANGEL.
>Put away your pride. Quickly, hide,
>before He finds out.

2ND GOOD ANGEL.
>Yes, when our Lord and Master sees
>His anger will be dreadful to behold.

2ND BAD ANGEL.
>I think you make a splendid sight.
>Stay: why do as you're told?

LUCIFER.
>So, my companions, if I look so fine
>And suit the part
>Do you think the job
>Is mine?

1ST BAD ANGEL.
>Yes, you shall lead from today.

1ST GOOD ANGEL.
>No, there is only one who rules. We won't obey.

LUCIFER.
>I am Lucifer, Master of Light!
>Monarch of all I survey:
>Now I'll test these wings
>in flight.

He tries to fly above GOD's *throne.* GOD *appears. We hear
the* Dies Irae *loud and threatening.* LUCIFER *is despatched by
aeriel runway. The* BAD ANGELS *tumble down the Keep.*
GOOD ANGELS *drive them across the Motte into Hellmouth.
Two masked* DEVILS *immediately rush out in torment. The
voices of the* BAD ANGELS *are heard.*

1ST DEVIL.
>Help, O help us!
>Now we have fallen from grace,
>gone from the highest Heaven
>into this awful place
>where none can save us. He who we thought so fine
>has fallen furthest of us all,
>deeper than any mine.

2ND DEVIL.
>Lost, all is lost.
Pride comes, they say, before a fall.
Our pride has cost
the biggest fall of all.
We were in Heaven, now we are left
outside. Locked out for evermore.
Lucifer, black angel once so bright
What is this place of pain
and endless night?

The DEVILS *disappear back into Hellmouth.*

Music. GOD *is back on his throne surrounded by* ANGELS.

GOD.
>Though I have filled my creation with living things
It doesn't seem complete. It needs one thing,
Someone to oversee it for me. I shall call him
Adam, make him upright and tall
in my own image.

He processes towards the Eden Stage, preceded by a
MUSICIAN *possibly playing* Veni Creator Spiritus *and*
followed by ANGELS. *The* MUSICIAN *goes over to Eden,*
GOD, *etc. Stop at Motte Stage.* ADAM *rises out of the trap as*
GOD *speaks the next.*

GOD.
>Into this clay I now infuse
the gift of life. Born of my shaping spirit
I form you complete and perfect
as from the potter's wheel.
Arise! Live in pleasure
in this place that I have made for you.
Manage it well for me. Make yourself free
of all I offer.

ADAM *yawns, eventually falls asleep, lying curled in front of*
trap.

>Sleep my newest creature, and I will fill
your head with brightest dreams.
How lonely it seems! All other things that
walk my world

I've given mates to help them multiply.
Can I deny
This pleasure to you also?

EVE *rises out of* ADAM's *body.* ADAM *awakes.*

ADAM.
Was I asleep? Did I dream you?

EVE.
I somehow seem to know you . . . did I dream you too?

GOD.
Adam, here is Eve, to partner you
and share your world, your duties
and your leisure. You shall live
in a place called Paradise. Do as you will
except for just one thing.

There is a tree grows there, the Tree of Life:
It is forbidden to you, Adam, and Eve
your wife. All fruits and flowers, flesh and fish
are yours to do with as you wish.
But remember the Tree:
Mark well the words from me.
Think on!

GOD *sends* ANGEL *across to Eden.*

ANGEL.
Come Eve, come Adam, into this garden
furnished for all your needs. Live here
in innocence but never forget
to thank the Lord who made you. Who asks
no recompense but one small thing:
Keep away from that Tree. All else
is free. Live here carefree as the day
but fear His anger if you disobey.

Exit ANGEL.

ADAM.
Eve, sister . . . woman . . . wife . . .
look at this garden, see this place
that He has made for us.

EVE.
>Adam, dear brother . . . husband . . .
>This is a place that truly might be called
>Paradise.

ADAM.
>All these varieties of trees and flowers
>Surely happiness will be ours
>in this place. I think I'll look around . . .

EVE.
>Yes, go on, love. Explore your
>new-found kingdom.
>I'll stay here and rest.

ADAM.
>Very well, you know best.
>But remember what the Angel said
>about the Tree.

EVE.
>Go, don't worry about me,
>I'm fine. I wouldn't dare
>upset our Maker.

>*Exit* ADAM. LUCIFER/SATAN *appears.*

SATAN.
>What a fearsome fate. Cast in dark dungeons
>for evermore. Me and my mates,
>my fellow rebels cast in the deepest pit.
>The happiness we lost
>He's given to this new creation, Man
>and Woman, now happy as we should be.
>A sight unbearable to me.
>Here she is, alone
>and open, perhaps, to temptation.
>I wonder . . . perhaps I might insinuate
>myself . . . in guise of a humble serpent
>my lies may sound more convincing . . .
>Revenge!

>*He moves to the Garden.* EVE *sees him.*

SATAN.
>Eve!
>Do not fear. I am a lowly creature, a serpent.

One of your humble servants. Here
to do your bidding. All this fruit
looks delicious. Aren't you hungry?
Don't you want to try some?

EVE.

They look and smell so good
I can hardly choose between them.

SATAN.

Yes, you're almost spoilt for choice.
(*Slyly*.) Mind you, this one here
looks particularly inviting . . .
. . . imagine biting into that.

EVE.

Not that one, no!
We've promised not to go
anywhere near it.

SATAN.

Why is this so?

EVE.

I don't know. Our Master
simply told us not to go
anywhere near.

SATAN.

With no reason?
And all this lovely fruit in season?

EVE.

No, He just warned of His great anger
if we disobeyed.

SATAN.

Eve, listen to me. I may be
only a humble serpent but I am wise
in the ways of this world so new to you.
He has warned you off this tree
because its fruit has a particular property.
Listen carefully. You and your Adam
are children, innocents, knowing
nothing. One bite of this fruit and you will
have Wisdom. There is no poison here,
only Knowledge. Knowledge of everything,

of good and bad, of all things in
this universe. Why do you think
He forbids you this treat?
Worries that you will eat
and know?

EVE.
I don't know. Tell me, wise creature.

SATAN.
Because He fears your knowledge.
With the help of this tree
you can be as wise, as powerful
as He: you, and Adam.
What a surprise for *him*, when he comes back.
Trust me . . .
                    . . . go on, try . . .

EVE.
I don't know . . .

SATAN.
Just a little bite . . .

EVE.
Well, nothing ventured, nothing gained,
I suppose . . . here goes . . .

*Hesitantly, she takes and bites the fruit. It tastes good. She eats
more.*

EVE.
Mmm. It's good.

SATAN (*who has been exulting in his triumph unseen by* EVE).
What did I tell you?
Now, try it on your husband.

He sneaks away, enter ADAM. *He sees her with the fruit.*

ADAM.
Eve, Eve, girl, what have you done?

EVE.
Don't worry, love, this fruit is good. Try some.

ADAM.
But we were told . . .

EVE.
>   . . . we were told
> not to eat the fruit because it brings
> great blessings. Knowledge, wisdom.
> We will know as much as Him
> Who made us. It's all true,
> the serpent told me. A wise creature,
> who means us well. We needn't tell,
> Adam, love, try some . . .

ADAM.
> Yes, it tastes good. And yet I feel
> strange. There's a change in me
> I feel . . .

He shivers, puts his hands instinctively over his genitals.

> . . . *naked* . . . and ashamed.

EVE (*trying to cover herself*).
>   Me too!

ADAM.
> It's as if I hadn't seen you before.

EVE.
> O Adam, forgive me.
> We never should have touched
> this tree.

ADAM.
> The fault was just as great with me.
> He warned us both. O Eve,
> let's leave this awful place. There are
> other corners of this garden
> That could shelter us.

EVE.
> We should cover ourselves. Perhaps
> some leaves will do for now.
> Come on. Let's slip away.

GOD.
> Adam! Adam!

ADAM.
> Yes . . . yes Lord?

GOD.
>Adam, you have disobeyed me,
>eaten from the Tree.

EVE.
>My Lord, it was me. My fault.
>A serpent spoke to me,
>so persuasively.

GOD.
>From now on I curse him and all his kind.
>Condemned to crawl forever,
>belly-down amid the mud and weeds.

>*With a cry* SATAN *falls prone. He crawls away.*

>Now Adam, and now you, Eve,
>who might have lived in innocence,
>in peace and plenty in this garden,
>take your new found knowledge,
>go out into the world, and work.
>Find food, make clothing for yourselves.

>*Loud sinister chorus of the* Dies Irae *again. The* ANGEL
>*expels them from the Garden. They exit miserably into the
>trees.*

ANGEL.
>Say goodbye to this enchanted place,
>Look your last upon its face.
>Go Adam, Eve leave here.
>You have fallen from His grace
>Go! In disgrace

A Man, A Woman and A Tree:

CHORUS.
>A man, a woman and a tree
>Symbol of immortality
>Symbol of our humanity
>A man, a woman and a tree

>This is the tree of knowledge
>This is the tree of sin
>This is the tree of passion
>The pattern must begin

A man, a woman and a tree
Symbol of immortality
The story's end will always be
A man, a woman and a tree

GOD and ANGELS process from Motte Stage left to Motte Stage right and off, passing GARCIO, CAIN's servant, dancing on the Keep Stage to band music.

*GARCIO.
Hello! Hello! Hello!
I'm Garcio. Gather round, listen and see,
You've heard of Jack the Lad,
Well I'm Jill the Lass!
And if you don't like it
You can kiss my ass!
Thank you!
My master, Cain, is a right good farmer,
and I'm his right-hand woman
(he even pays me when he can).
I'm off. I've got better things to do
than talk to you.

Exit GARCIO. Enter CAIN in tractor drawing trailer. GOD is seated in the back. It stops by the Central Cross.

CAIN.
Well bugger me, it's gone again
I don't know why I bother, I really don't
Come on damn you
Go.

Engine coughs and dies.

Fit for the knackers' yard, this.
Just look at the state of it!
Scrap. That's all it's good for
Scrap!
Garcio!
Where are you ragarse? Have I got to do
everything on my own?

GARCIO (*aside*).
God's curse on folk who do nowt but moan.

---

* See p 97 for alternative dialogue if Garcio is to be played as a boy.

CAIN.
    Have I to do it all myself? Didn't you hear
    me shout?

GARCIO.
    You're always shouting. All right,
    let's get it turned about. Come on
    Let's go. Get your arse in gear
    Come on, come on
    (*Aside.*) Mind you, it'd go better if he had
    it serviced from time to time.

CAIN.
    I heard that line.
    Just watch it, buggerlugs!

    Slaps him. GARCIO *slaps him back.*

GARCIO.
    And you watch it, too!

CAIN (*taken aback*).
    Listen, I'm the boss, don't forget.

GARCIO.
    And I'm the lass who gives as good as she gets.

CAIN.
    All right, all right, let's get on.*

ABEL.
    Cain! Cain!

CAIN.
    Oh, God
    That's all we need. My precious brother,
    Come to preach again. He's a right pain.
    What is it, brother dear? Spit it out
    and make yourself scarce. Frankly,
    you're a pain in the arse.

ABEL.
    Brother, brother, why do you carry on so?
    Don't you know I want to help you.

* Alternative dialogue ends here.

CAIN.

>Then give us a hand with this bloody plough.
>Let's have a bit of brotherly help,
>right now. Or piss off back to the Dales
>and leave me in peace.

ABEL.

>Cain, lad, another time I'd be pleased to help you.
>Today there's more important things to do.
>We pay our tithe to Him who gave us life,
>prosperity, as our father Adam taught us.
>To give back to Him one-tenth
>of what He's given us. Come on, Cain,
>let's go and make the sacrifice.

CAIN.

>Very nice, drop everything,
>stop ploughing, and give away a share
>of my hard work to someone who doesn't care
>what happens to me. When everyone's corn
>was full and ripe, my field was half empty.
>Talk about plenty. Who sent me
>rain when I didn't need it
>and drought when I needed rain?
>And here we are again,
>having to fork out a share
>of what we haven't got.

ABEL.

>Look, we must make the sacrifice
>or risk His anger at our ingratitude.
>Let's not be rude or ungracious
>to Him that made us. Who can tell
>next year you might do well.
>Who knows what might be in store,
>full barns and more.
>Come on, put a brave face on it.

CAIN.

>Oh, very well, let's get it over with.

>*They go to the Central Cross to make the sacrifice.* ABEL *sets
>fire to his bundle, which burns fiercely. He kneels.*

ABEL.

>Great Father, Maker of Heaven and Earth
>Take this humble rent from a grateful

tenant, in heartfelt thanks for all
that You have sent.

CAIN.

All right, all right, don't make a meal of it.
Come on, let's get it over with.
Lord, I really can't afford
to give You all this. Let's see . . .
One for You and one for me
One for You and two for me
One for You and three for me . . .
Would You like a tithe
of all the thistles and briars,
nettles and ivy I've harvested?
No? Oh well . . . one for You . . . no . . . not that one . . .

He takes back a large sheaf and puts out a tiny one instead.

ABEL.

Brother, brother, you can't just pick and choose!

CAIN.

Why not? What have I got to lose?

ABEL.

God's goodwill, that's what.
Come on, think on, lad.

CAIN.

There, that's my lot. Let's get it done with.

He tries to set fire to his tithe. Black smoke billows out.

(*Spluttering.*) Urgh! God's teeth!
Kiss the Devil's arse!
Argh! Argh! Burn, you bastard, burn!

He blows on the fire. Even more smoke billows into his face.

Urgh! What a smell!
Like Old Nick's farted
in Hell.
It's always the same.
Yours burned all right, so why not
mine? I suppose yours is superior,
you sanctimonious swine.

GOD *appears from amidst the hay bales on the trailer.*

GOD.

    Cain, why do you treat your brother like this?
    Why can't you make a decent sacrifice,
    like his? To them that give will be given.
    This investment will be repaid a hundredfold
    in Heaven. (*Exit* GOD.)

CAIN.

    A voice! I'm sure I heard a voice!
    (*To audience*.) Did you hear it?
    Come on, let's go.
    God doesn't want to know.

ABEL.

    Cain, don't say that. He loves you
    just as much as me. Just trust Him,
    you'll see.

SATAN *appears and watches the rest of the scene.*

CAIN.

    Oh aye, yes. Just look at that pathetic fag-end
    of a fire. *Yours* burned clear and bright.
    Mine was like a burning sheepshite. Oh, yes,
    We all know whose side He's on.
    Right! I've had enough! See if He
    can get you out of this one!

He seizes a spanner and smashes it down on ABEL's *head. We
hear the* Dies Irae *chords again.*

ABEL (*dying*).
               Vengeance!

GOD.

    Cain! Cain!

CAIN.

    It's that voice again. Yes? I'm here.

GOD.

    And where's your brother?

CAIN.

    Perhaps in Hell. Or sleeping.
    He's a very heavy sleeper. Who can tell?
    I'm not my brother's keeper.

GOD.

His blood cries out for vengeance.
Now hear this curse: a fate far worse
than death. From now on you will walk the Earth
despised and shunned by all. Marked
for ever. The first murderer. Cursed.

Exit GOD.

*CAIN.

Very well, I'm cursed. So be it.
I'll keep myself to myself.
Where's that useless cow, God rot her!
Garcio! Where have you got to now?

Enter GARCIO. CAIN *cuffs her about the ears.*

CAIN.

Come here while I hit you, scumbag.
What do you mean by it? You're never here when
you're wanted. There's work to do.
A pit to be dug.

GARCIO.

A pit? Round here?

CAIN.

Didn't I make myself clear?

GARCIO (*sees the body*).

B-but it's y-your brother Abel dead!

CAIN.

Well said. How truly observant of you.
Now, get rid of him.

GARCIO.

But . . . What will happen if they find him?
They'll blame me too, as well as you.

CAIN.

Oh, for God's sake.
All right.
If it'll keep you quiet I'll proclaim
your innocence for all to hear.
Go on, introduce me.

* See p. 98 for alternative dialogue.

GARCIO.
>Oyez, Oyez, Oyez!
>Hear ye, Hear ye, Hear ye!

CAIN.
>I solemnly proclaim . . .

GARCIO (*mocking him*).
>I'm a villain. Cain's the name . . .

CAIN.
>. . . That this girl you know as Garcio . . .

GARCIO.
>. . . a handsome lass as you well know . . .

CAIN.
>. . . is innocent of any crime, now or before . . .

GARCIO.
>. . . *He's* done enough to hang himself, and more . . .

CAIN.
>. . . and is innocent of any sin.

GARCIO.
>. . . it's *him* who's done his brother in.

CAIN.
>There!

GARCIO (*mocking*).
>There!

CAIN.
>Now, enough of this tomfoolery.
>Let's see you shift this plough. Go on,
>get off with you.

GARCIO.
>Goodbye one and all. I've got to go.
>God's blessing from your good friend Garcio!

Exit GARCIO *driving tractor. As* CAIN *says the next he is led away by* SATAN.*

CAIN.
>Now I must leave the haunts of man
>and hide myself in shadows. Satan

* Alternative dialogue ends here.

my only friend. A weary way to wend.
Farewell.

The COMPANY *come through the audience orgiastically,
finally exiting leaving* NOAH *praying on the Keep Stage
surrounded by domestic activity.*

GOD.

Don't think that I don't know
what they're doing once again.
Why, of all creatures that I have made,
should these humans trouble me so much?
Why do they plague me so? I don't know
what to do with them. They'd try
the patience of a Saint.

NOAH.

Lord,
I have grown old watching all around me
fall into evil ways. Who but me
still prays to You? Who makes
a sacrifice? Greed and Envy,
corruption and vice abound, yet
all around me seem to profit;
they don't seem to struggle, like me,
to make ends meet. Truly, Lord,
Your people have fallen from grace.
I only wish to see Your face
in Heaven when I go.

GOD.

Only this one here,
Noah, pays me any respect. He and his family
live in honourable poverty, yet never fail
to worship me. I'm sick and fed up
with the rest of them. I'll contrive a flood; great seas
indescribable torrents will cover the Earth:
the waters will take back the land,
and all will drown and die. My punishment
will exclude no-one, beggar or King,
child or pensioner, peasant or nobility.
All but he, this good man, Noah.
Let's start again with him, and his family.
He'll listen if the message comes direct

from me. (*He leans across to talk to* NOAH.)
Now listen to me
Noah, and think on. Things have gone
too far. There's going to be a flood, a storm
the like of which you've never seen.
You must build a boat,
a giant ship, take you and yours a trip
upon the waters. Build it good and strong –
let's see – say 50 cubits wide and 300 long
and 30 high: enough to fit a lot of animals
inside. Plenty of pitch to make it waterproof.
A good stout roof, a couple of dozen stalls to
house the creatures. Great and small, you'll
take all with you. And don't forget fodder for the
birds and beasts. And you and yours, of course
Forty days and forty nights at least
it's going to rain.

GOD *walks up, sits on Platform Stage and watches.*

NOAH.
Who can this be who can forestall fate,
by the Holy Trinity?

GOD.
Precisely. One in Three, indivisible;
the Lord your Master: that's me.

NOAH.
Forgive me, Lord, I never thought
You'd appear to anyone as unworthy
as me.

GOD.
You are a good man, Noah, in a wicked world:
go with my blessing. You
and your children have a chance
to start anew. (*Exit* GOD.)

NOAH.
What amazing news! Oh, well,
better get to work at once. There's more
than enough to do. Oh, Lord
What'll the missus say when I tell her?
She's a bit of a shrew, to say the least.

She's not afraid of man nor beast.
Oh, heck, how am I going to break it to her?

FAMILY *unfreezes,* CHILDREN *exit to ark.*

UXOR.
>   And what time do you call this?
>   Do you think that I've got nothing better to do
>   than hang around all day and wait
>   for you?

NOAH.
>   Er – how are you, love?

UXOR.
>   None the better for seeing you. Here you are
>   Coming home empty-handed again, I see.
>   How do you expect me to make do with nothing?
>   Other men come home with plenty. Why are you
>   so hopeless? (*To Audience.*) Men! Aren't they a trial?
>   The Virgin herself must have suffered.
>   But no-one's tried like me. As you can see.
>   I'll give him something for his troubles
>   before the day's out. And it won't be supper . . .

NOAH.
>   Listen . . .

UXOR.
>   I'm fed up with listening. *You* listen . . .

NOAH.
>   Listen, you old ratbag, for God's sake.
>   Let me get a word in edgewise.

UXOR.
>   Who do you think you're talking to,
>   You great heap of sheepspooh?

NOAH.
>   You! (*Slaps her.*) You old bat!
>   Try *that* for size! (*Slaps her again.*)

UXOR.
>   Right! (*Slaps him.*)
>   I'll give as good as I get
>   from you! (*Slaps him again.*) You little worm!

They belabour each other, Punch-and-Judy style.

NOAH (*breathless*).

Listen, listen, we've more
important things to do. I don't know
about you, but my arms ache.

UXOR.

There's more than my arms aching. I can
tell you.

NOAH (*grudging admiration*).

By, you've got a heavy hand on you.

UXOR (*equally grudging*).

You, too.

NOAH.

Now, listen, there's a lot to do. I've got
to learn carpentry and trigonometry,
joinery and astronomy,
all in the name of the blessed Trinity. I've got
to build a boat. A big boat. And soon.

UXOR.

What for? Is this another of your daft schemes?
Who dreamed this one up?

NOAH.

The Lord himself commanded me.
He said there's going to be a flood . . .

UXOR.

Hm. We'll see.

NOAH.

Well, at least pray for me.

UXOR.

I wouldn't pray for you
if you were the last man on Earth.
Get off and build your ship:
I've got proper work to do.

*She gets on with her spinning. He crosses to area between
Baddies' Stage and Queen's Tower where the SONS and
WIVES have brought on a truck with the deconstructed Ark.
They build the Ark. Music during this, punctuated by
increasing thunder noises made by entire cast – thunder sheets
etc. Then business of herding and loading the animals,*

provisions etc. Meanwhile UXOR *is still on Motte Stage doing her housework. Thunder, lightning, rain, pouring water effects.* NOAH *and the others call out to her: the ship is finished. She ignores them. Finally,* NOAH *comes to Area Two to fetch her.*

NOAH.

Come on, woman, what's the matter with you?

UXOR.

I've got things to do.

NOAH.

If you don't hurry up it'll be the last
thing you do. Can't you hear it out
there?

Storm noises increase.

UXOR.

I don't care. Anyway, you're not getting me
in *that* thing.

NOAH.

What?

UXOR.

That great big ugly thing you've built.
Cooped up like a chicken for God knows how
long! *And* all those smelly animals! Catch
me! Anyway, if God wanted me to live in
water, he'd have given me fins and a tail.

NOAH.

He should have given you horns and a tail,
more like.

UXOR (*to audience*).

Listen to him. Men. They're all
the same. Think they know it all. I'll be
glad when he's six feet under. The best thing
about marriage is looking forward to being a
widow.

NOAH.

Now look here . . .

UXOR.

And you look here . . .

Chorus of 'Come on Mother' etc from the Ark.

NOAH.
Will you do as you're told! (*Shaking her.*)
I'm fed up to the back teeth with you.

UXOR (*pushing him away*).
You won't have any back
teeth when I've finished with you!

NOAH.
Sez who?

UXOR.
Sez me.

NOAH.
Says you?

UXOR.
Says me.

Terrific Punch-and-Judy set-to again. Their battle is only ended by a huge clap of thunder and lightning. Pouring rain. Chorus of 'Mother, Dad, hurry up' etc from the Ark.

NOAH.
Hurry up, woman, you'll drown. (*Exits to Ark.*)

UXOR.
All right, all right, hold your horses.

She's gathering up her possessions. Another gigantic thunder clap. She's drenched with water. Gathering up her skirts and shrieking she legs it to the Ark. They haul her in, unceremoniously. We see the business of their journey behind the next song.

Animals'/Children's Song:

Seven days and seven nights,
Never stopping, day or night.
Rain till the rivers join the sea,
Covering up the tallest tree;
Rain till all the valleys fill,
Covering up the highest hill.
Seven days and seven nights
Never stopping, day or night.

Forty days and forty nights,
Sailing on by day and night.

This small family in a boat,
The only living thing afloat;
Water, water everywhere,
The only creatures God has spared.
Forty days and forty nights,
Sailing on by day and night.

NOAH (*spoken*).

Weeks and months without a stop,
Waiting till the waters drop.
Send a dove to look for land,
Now she's back on Noah's hand.
Here's her prize: a tiny leaf
Taken from an olive tree.
Weeks and months without a stop;
Suddenly, the waters drop.

Finally they emerge from the Ark, ANIMALS *and all. Whole*
cast sings an Anthem of Thanksgiving. Effect of a rainbow.

ALL.

While the Earth remains
Seedtime and harvest,
Cold and heat
Summer and winter
And day and night
Shall not cease.

While we live in peace
Seedtime and harvest
Cold and heat
Summer and winter
And day and night
All things will live

While God forgives
Seedtime and harvest
Cold and heat
Summer and winter
And day and night
Shall not cease

Exit ALL.

Interval.

Music. GOD *appears on the Keep.* ABRAHAM *on the Motte, faces audience.*

GOD.
> So I saved Noah from the Flood.
> A good man. And his wife (a bit
> of a rough diamond, I admit)
> and his children. And now *their* children:
> a mixed bunch, all in all. They're at it
> again. They haven't learnt a thing
> since the Fall. Except this one,
> Abraham, and he's getting on. I wonder
> if he's really good. Let's put him under
> a bit of stress . . . a really stiff test
> should show us what he's made of.
> (*Thinks.*) That's it. Abraham!

ABRAHAM.
> Who is it? Who called me?

GOD.
> You don't know me but I know you.
> You don't see me but I can see
> right through you, Abraham.
> I am your Lord and Master.

ABRAHAM (*falling to the ground*).
> Lord, tell me what I
> can do to serve You. Anything, just ask.

GOD.
> There is something you might do for me
> a small matter of a sacrifice.

ABRAHAM.
> A sacrifice, Lord? Simple enough,
> and given willingly. I won't stint You,
> Lord, You'll see.

Lights up on ISAAC *playing on a swing on Motte Stage.*

GOD.
> Then this is my command. Take your son,
> Isaac, to the mountains of Moriah,
> the Land of Vision. There you will build a fire
> and sacrifice him. No indecision.

A gift freely offered, and freely given.
What do you say?

ABRAHAM.
What can I say? My offer stands. His life
is in Your hands. I am old and grey
and he is the comfort of my declining years;
tears come to me at the thought of losing him.
Yet I will obey, Lord. I'll away
and find him, ready for the journey.

Exit GOD. ISAAC *has stopped playing and crosses to*
ABRAHAM.

ISAAC.
Hello, Father. Had a good day?

ABRAHAM.
A heavy one, I fear. Listen, forget your play,
prepare yourself. We're going away.
On a journey.

ISAAC.
A journey? Where to?

ABRAHAM.
A distant place. Moriah, the Land of Vision
high in the mountains. There we must make
a sacrifice. The Lord commands it.
You must go as I say.

Exit ISAAC, *excited. Collects bags and travels to Central*
Cross.

ABRAHAM.
Of all the journeys, all the weary ways
I've travelled, these three days
will be the darkest. Yet who am I
to question orders: what is my sorrow
to His, who suffers for us all?

ABRAHAM *crosses to the Central Cross as* ISAAC *prepares*
the fire.

ISAAC.
Father, everything's ready. The fire's ready to
light, the knife's laid out. But where's the

sacrifice? What beast must we kill today? Is it
something special?

ABRAHAM.
Very special.

ISAAC.
And valuable?

ABRAHAM.
More than I can tell.

ISAAC.
Then where is it? I can't solve this puzzle.
Where is it? I can't see . . .

*He looks round, sees his father's face. It sinks in, slowly.
Horror.*

. . . O Father! Not me?

ABRAHAM.
It has to be.

ISAAC.
But why?

ABRAHAM.
It's not my decision. The Lord has asked
for my dearest, most treasured possession.
I would have given anything; jewels, my house,
your mother, my wife, my own life. Anything.
He has asked for the one thing that tears my
heart apart. Face the knife and pray that He
will welcome you in Heaven.

ISAAC.
O Father, spare me. I don't want to die.
Please . . .

ABRAHAM.
On your knees. Look up to Him above.
His love, though mysterious, is greater
than mine. I love you more than anything.
Your brief life will carry on in
Paradise.

ISAAC.
If you can't spare me, then . . . say goodbue
to my little brother. I'll miss the others.

And kiss my mother for me. Tell her I love her.
Now I must prepare.

He lays himself on the funeral pyre.

The knife gleams against the sky
and I must die. Why should it be?
Father, why have you forsaken me?

ABRAHAM *moves to him, knife held high, prepares.* BOY
SOPRANO'S VOICE *is heard singing.*

BOY'S VOICE.
    Father, Father
    Why have you forsaken me?
    Please don't leave me
    Here to wait in agony
    One touch of your hand
    And you could set me free
    Father, Father
    Why have you forsaken me?

GOD *appears, lifts his hand.* ABRAHAM *freezes.*

GOD'S VOICE.
    He's done it. He's passed the test.
    Abraham, and all his family
    will be blessed. I will smile
    upon their every enterprise.
    (*To* ANGEL.) Go Angels, release him from his word.

Verse Two of the song while ANGELS *advance down each
duckboard and approach the Cross.* ABRAHAM *and* ISAAC
still frozen. The ANGELS *raise their wings.* ABRAHAM *and*
ISAAC *move as the* ANGEL *speaks.*

BOY'S VOICE.
    Father, Father
    Why have you forsaken me?
    Please don't leave me
    Lying here in misery
    If you love your son
    Then take the knife from me
    Father, Father
    Why have you forsaken me?

ANGEL.

>Abraham, you are released. Spare this lamb
>from the knife. We'll find a four legged one
>to sacrifice. This the Lord God commands.
>Your decision was enough: the deed we'll take
>for granted. Go, with His blessing.

>ABRAHAM *and* ISAAC *embrace each other and exit, escorted
>by* ANGELS, *accompanied by a* MUSICIAN – *possibly one of
>the* ANGELS.

>*God Theme.* GOD *appears, speaks.*

GOD.

>There is a shepherd lad called Moses
>One of the Israelites held captive in the land
>of Egypt. He doesn't know it yet
>but he is born to greatness.
>It is he that I have chosen
>to set my people free:
>I think I'll speak to him
>Out of this tree.

>MOSES *appears cycling on the Motte. A bramble bush bursts
>into flames.* GOD'S VOICE *comes from it.*

GOD.

>Moses!

MOSES.

>Y-Yes?

GOD.

>Moses, I am the Lord your Master.
>I watched your rescue from the waters, saw you
>brought up by Pharaoh's daughter, supervised
>your escape from slaughter, and now
>your path has led to me, speaking
>from this sacred tree. Stay put. You may not
>see me face to face. Take off your shoes,
>this is a Holy place.

MOSES.

>Lord, what do You want of me?

GOD.

>I need you. You are to be my messenger.

MOSES.
>Messenger?

GOD.
>To Pharaoh. Tell him to let my chosen
>ones go.

MOSES.
>What, me? I couldn't go to Pharaoh with
>words like that, Lord. He'd kill me.

GOD.
>Patience, Moses, patience.
>Tell your people to bide their time
>Their slavery will soon be over.
>Meanwhile announce yourself
>to Pharaoh as my messenger. He'll want
>some trifling proof of authenticity, no doubt.
>Just take your staff and throw it on the ground,
>then pick it up again. That'll convince him.
>You'll be surprised.

MOSES.
>Well . . . if You say so, Lord . . .

We hear a chorus singing 'Go Down Moses'.

GOD.
>Tell him to let my people go
>into the wilderness and worship me
>and live in peace and plenty.
>You shall lead them, Moses, to a far place
>flowing with milk and honey.
>Oh, and tell Pharaoh if he disobeys
>he'll rue the day he was born. On his head
>be it. Go, then, Moses, trusty messenger.

The bush stops burning. MOSES *goes to* PHARAOH's *palace.
Fanfare. Arrival of* PHARAOH'S COURT *on Baddies' Stage.*

PHARAOH.
>I am Pharaoh, King of Kings.
>Look on my works, Almighty, and despair.
>My word ranges farther than the eye can see.
>All men bow down and worship me.
>All, that is, except one paltry tribe.

Children of Israel, they call themselves.
They worship a strange god, and say they're
The Chosen Ones. And they multiply,
breeding quicker than they die.
Chosen ones, indeed. Soon there'll be nothing left
to choose from. I'll make them toe the line.

SOLDIER.

Your Majesty, one of the Israelites wants to
petition you. Claims to be a spokesman for
whatever god it is they worship.

PHARAOH.

Oh, very well, show him in.

MOSES.

Great Pharaoh, the Lord God of Israel
wishes to speak to you through me. I am
His Messenger.

PHARAOH.

And a pretty tatty one, too. You smell
of sheep. Which god is this?

MOSES.

Our Lord, the only true God.

PHARAOH.

They all say that. Get on with it, then.

MOSES.

He asked me to show you this rod.

*Throws staff to the ground. It turns into a snake. He is as
astonished as* PHARAOH. *Gingerly he picks it up by the tail:
it turns into a staff.*

PHARAOH.

Yes. A good trick, certainly.
But I've got court magicians who I'm sure
could do as well. But I'll accept you as a
messenger from some strange deity. Now tell me
what is this message that's so important?

MOSES.

The Lord my God says set my people free.
Let them go into the wilderness and seek a place

where they can live in peace and worship me.
We wish you no harm, just leave us be.

PHARAOH.
The impudence! The nerve! Set you free?
You can go and tell your precious tribe
I've doubled their workload. That'll show them.

MOSES.
That is your final word on the matter?

PHARAOH.
I've said enough. I refuse to discuss it
any further. Take him away.

MOSES.
Very well, on your head be it. You and your
people will live to rue this day.

*A procession of plague banners in front of stage. The first six
plagues clear the audience from the area between the stage and
the Cross where the* CHORUS OF ISRAELITES *are.*
PHARAOH *and his retinue become increasingly agitated.*
MOSES *and* PHARAOH *respond to* CHORUS.

CHORUS OF ISRAELITES.
Blood.
Lakes and rivers,
Pools and streams,
All turned to
Blood.
The Earth stinks.
Blood to wash in,
Blood to drink.
The beaches are awash with
Blood.

MOSES.
And still he will not let my people be.

PHARAOH.
And still I will not set his people free.

CHORUS.
Lice.
The tiniest of predators.
Infesting the land.

Numerous as grains of sand.
Dogs and cats,
Humans and beasts
Driven to despair.

MOSES.

And still he will not let my people be.

PHARAOH.

And still I will not set his people free.

CHORUS.

Flies.
The spawn of Beezlebub.
A black airforce covering everything.
Courtroom and market,
Garden and schoolroom
Filled with their buzzing.

MOSES.

And still he will not let my people be.

PHARAOH.

And still I will not set his people free.

CHORUS.

Boils
Great pustules,
Giant chilblains rack the populace with pain.
No-one is spared.
No doctor can cure them.
No priest can charm them away.
They're here to stay.

MOSES.

And still he will not let my people be.

PHARAOH.

And still I will not set his people free.

CHORUS.

Hail, all conquering hail.
The skies rain frozen madness.
No tree, no plant can stand against it.
Neither man nor beast dare venture forth.
The cold, unforgiving rain.

MOSES.

And still he will not let my people be.

PHARAOH.

And still I will not set his people free.

CHORUS.

Last the locust,
But not the least.
Greediest of all natural beasts,
gobbling all before it.
Not a leaf,
Not a stem,
Not a berry left behind.

MOSES.

And still he will not let my people be.

PHARAOH.

And still I will not set his people free.

MOSES.

Now, proud princeling, do you bow
before the Lord God of Israel? Now you will
agree to set my people free?

PHARAOH.

Yes . . . No . . . I won't let them go.

MOSES.

Very well. On your head be it.

*The plague banners are laid on the stage as the final plague
arrives.*

CHORUS.

Plague, plague, plague, plague . . .
Steals in the night like a burglar.
Creeps unseen unto the marriage bed,
Between lovers, children's cots:
No-one escapes its dark embrace.
Swiftest of all,
Plague.

MOSES.

Now will you let our people be?
Now will you set our people free?

PHARAOH.

Yes, yes, take this terrible curse
away from me. Just go!

MOSES (*to* CHORUS *and audience*).

Brothers, sisters,
we are released from bondage. All is well.
But we must hurry. He'll soon change his mind
when things get better. We must trust in God.
He will part the Red Sea, make a passage
free for all of us. See, the waters move
at His command.

Go Down Moses:

When Israel was in Egypt's land,
Let my people go!
Oppressed so hard they could not stand,
Let my people go!
Go down, Moses,
Way down in Egypt's land,
Tell ol' Pharaoh,
Let my people go!

Thus spake the Lord, bold Moses said,
Let my people go!
If not, I'll strike your first-born dead,
Let my people go!
Go down, Moses,
Way down in Egypt's land,
Tell ol' Pharaoh,
Let my people go!

Ol' Pharaoh thought he had us fast,
Let my people go!
But we broke his chains at last,
Let my people go!
Go down, Moses,
Way down in Egypt's land,
Tell ol' Pharaoh,
Let my people go!

The CHORUS *becomes the Red Sea, holding material and
running. They split so that* MOSES *and* BANNER CARRIERS
– now ISRAELITES *– can pass through them.*

PHARAOH.
After them. No-one must escape.
Take your revenge for all our suffering.
After them, quick.

The ISRAELITES *are followed by* PHARAOH *and his* COURT. *Martial music falling apart into chaos as the sea swallows them and sweeps the* COURT *away – towards changing area.*

GOD *and* GABRIEL *have watched the proceedings from the Central Cross.*

GOD.
　　I am the word. And the word was the World,
　　and everything in it. And, crown of my creation,
　　mankind. Woman and man together
　　set to live in Paradise, cast out and cursed by
　　me, for eating from the Tree of Life.
　　Time now, perhaps, to think of forgiveness.
　　I will create a son to walk among men
　　In human form, the word made flesh
　　Come to redeem their ancient sin,
　　A man, born of woman, but Son of God.
　　Now is the time. I need a virgin girl,
　　a woman who has known no man. Gabriel!
　　Find me a woman who is wise and virtuous,
　　pure and virginal, to bear a son for me.

GABRIEL.
　　Master, there is one such woman,
　　living in a place called Nazareth,
　　in Galilee. Even though married to an older man,
　　she has kept her virginity. She saves herself
　　for the love of you, Lord. She spends her days
　　in worship, and has vowed no man shall touch her.
　　Pure as a vase of crystal.

GOD.
　　Pure as crystal . . . then we shall fill
　　that vessel with light, and life. Go,
　　tell her the good news, that she will
　　be filled with the Holy Spirit.
　　The child will be a boy and they will call Him
　　Jesus: He who will save them from sin.
　　Go, Gabriel, tell her I have chosen her
　　amongst all women.

MARY *lighting a fire at home (Keep Stage).* GABRIEL *goes to her.*

CHORUS.
>A man, a woman and a tree
>Symbol of immortality
>Symbol of our humanity
>A man, a woman and a tree
>
>This is the tree of knowledge
>This is the tree of sin
>This is the tree of passion
>The pattern must begin
>
>A man, a woman and a tree
>Symbol of immortality
>The story's end will always be
>A man, a woman and a tree

GABRIEL.
>Hail Mary full of grace,
>pure of body, fairest of face.
>You are chosen amongst all women
>to do the Lord's work.

MARY.
>Who are you?
>What kind of creature,
>come with this strange news?

GABRIEL.
>I am Gabriel, sent by the Lord to choose
>the vessel of salvation. A child
>born to redeem man's ancient sin. Within
>you the seed of the Lord's will.

MARY.
>A child? But I have lain with no man,
>not even my husband. Pure as first snow,
>waiting for His grace.

GABRIEL.
>And so you will remain. Without a stain
>upon that virgin whiteness. A child in your womb
>conceived without sin. He who creates life's
>mysteries has caused this paradox: a child
>conceived by the Holy Spirit. Your body
>a vessel to receive His son, who you will call
>Jesus.

A lighting/sound effect to suggest the Holy Spirit entering her.

MARY.
> What marvels! What mysteries!
> Already I can feel a change in me,
> Something filling me with light,
> and life (*On her knees.*)
> Thank you, Lord, for choosing
> this unworthy woman as Your bride.
> Chosen to bear Your child inside me.
> And thank you, Gabriel,
> messenger of joy.

Exit GABRIEL. The situation starts to sink in. JOSEPH *enters.*

> Oh, Heavens! What am I going to tell my husband?
> Er . . . Joseph, dear . . .

JOSEPH.
> Yes, my love?

MARY.
> I've . . . er . . . got some news . . . something to tell
> you . . .

JOSEPH.
> If it's good news, don't delay.

MARY.
> Oh, yes, it's good news . . . it's just that . . . well,
> I'm . . .

JOSEPH.
> You're what? Come on, out with it?

MARY.
> I'm pregnant. I'm going to have a baby.

JOSEPH.
> Pregnant? A baby?
> Well, one thing's certain: it's nowt to do with me.

MARY.
> There, you see, you've misunderstood me completely.

JOSEPH.
> I think I understand only too well. You tell me
> you're expecting. That means only one thing;
> you've never let me touch you; and anyway I'm

too old to: You've obviously found someone new
to pleasure you.

MARY (*tearful*).
                    But you don't understand.
No-one has slept with me
I'm as virgin as the day I met you.

JOSEPH (*sarcastic*).
                    A miracle! That's it!
Or you've been laid by a ghost.

MARY.
Well . . . a sort of ghost. The Spirit of God
has come to live inside me. His son
will be born to do great things.

JOSEPH.
That's great. Just great. What'll I tell them
in nine months' time? It's a ghost's not mine?

MARY.
Oh, Joseph . . .

She retires, sits in a heap sobbing.

JOSEPH (*to audience*).
                    Well, tell me, what would *you* do?
Would you accept a cock-and-bull tale
like that? A fat lot of sympathy I'll get.
An old man married to a lovely young girl,
always praying, looking as if butter wouldn't melt
in her mouth. And now she's up the chute.
Good for a laugh, that one. My wife? Oh, yes,
she's pregnant with the Holy Spirit. Oh, she's
still untouched, I'm sure. Nature never took
its course. What an actress, they'll say, what a fool.
Do you know I married her straight from school.
Her heart wasn't in it, though. She only wanted
to be married to the Lord. But they said
I should have a wife, so they paired me off
with Mary. I suppose it got her off their hands.
Lucky really, I suppose. Prettiest of the lot,
she was. A kind and loving nature . . . but none of
that, if you know what I mean. Clean. Neat.
A good cook. Hardly surprising someone of her

looks would stray. But I can't face them, I
can't. I couldn't bear their laughter.
Best just go. And yet
I love her so.

Sadly he prepares to depart. GABRIEL appears.

GABRIEL.

Joseph, Joseph, what are you thinking of?
What are these doubts? If you really love her,
you'd believe her story. As a matter of fact,
it's true. She's been with no-one. The Lord
Himself has chosen her to bear His only son.
She is the chosen one amongst all women. She
remains pure and true.
Oh, Joseph, the fault is not with her, but with you.

*Exit GABRIEL. JOSEPH goes to MARY, embraces her, comes
forward holding her to him.*

JOSEPH.

Mary my love, how can you ever forgive me?
An angel came, just when I was about to leave you.
Oh my love, I'm sorry. From now on I'll be a
model husband and father. I'll look after you,
and Him. Cater to your every whim.

MARY.

Dearest, there's nothing to forgive. The man
doesn't live who wouldn't take the news as you
did. Here, give us your hand. We will be the
happiest family in the land. But what of the
journey you must undertake? You'll have to make
it soon. It's almost census-time.

JOSEPH.

Yes. It seems to come round quicker every year.
Listen, my dear, you can't stay here alone. Not
now. We'll go to Bethlehem together. Will you
be fit to travel?

MARY.

Fit and feeling better than I've ever felt,
my love. This gift's more precious than
anything the taxman dreams of.

JOSEPH.

> Then I'll go and get things ready.
> Rest here awhile.

Exit JOSEPH. *Lights down except on* MARY. *She sings.*

MARY.

> My soul magnifies the Lord
> For He has chosen me, lowest of the lowly,
> and now all generations will bless me:
> my spirit rejoices in God my Saviour.
>
> My soul magnifies the Lord
> He has shown great strength, He has shown great mercy,
> turned away the rich and fed the needy:
> my spirit rejoices in God my Saviour.
>
> My soul magnifies the Lord.
> He has scattered the proud and exalted the humble,
> guided His children lest they stumble:
> My spirit rejoices in God my Saviour.

Light out on her. JOSEPH *returns. Together they begin their journey from the Motte Stage towards Eden. Music for this, perhaps an instrumental of* Magnificat. *'Star' effect (laser) on.*

1ST KING *enters, on horseback, led by* RETAINER, *the noise of his arrival interrupting music. He stops at the Central Cross where he will be joined by the other two.*

1ST KING.

> Many weary miles from home
> and still some way to go, I fear.
> The star that beckoned me here
> seems near, yet far. A companion
> for this journey would lighten the way.
> I'll stay here awhile.

Enter 2ND KING *with* RETINUE.

2ND KING.

> I have followed this strange light
> over desert and mountains,
> day and night. Somehow
> it calls to me. I can't rest

until I see the meaning of
this prophecy.

1ST KING.
Greetings, fellow traveller.
I have come many miles
following this wonder. Tell me,
are you also under its spell?

2ND KING.
Yes, I have travelled far
to unravel the meaning
of this star.

1ST KING.
Let's ride together, then. My name is Caspar,
Caspar of Saba. Astronomers and soothsayers
assure me that this light in the sky
foretells the birth of a great Prince.

2ND KING.
Wise men in Tarsus tell me the same.
Melchior's my name. They say
He'll be a Prince amongst Princes,
greatest of all potentates.

Enter 3RD KING *with* RETINUE.

3RD KING.
Why does it call me on, this bright star?
Why have I come from my country,
my people, to follow this sign
in the sky? My only ambition now
to see the King whose birth was
foretold to me.

The 3RD KING *and* RETINUE *have not caught up*.

3RD KING.
My lords, something tells me
we are well-met. Do I take it
we follow the same road, seeking
the same goal? I seek a Princeling
sent without sin to rule us all.
This will fulfil an ancient prophecy.
I am Balthasar, King of Arabia,

a land far from here. Sirs,
may I join you on your journey?

1ST KING.
Certainly. Three's company, they say.

2ND KING.
Soon we'll enter the Kingdom of the Jews:
we must pay respects to Herod, the ruler,
tell him the good news.

3RD KING.
I agree: a common courtesy, and prudent.
We shall require safe-conduct through this land.

Fanfare. Lights up on HEROD *in his court on Area One.
Music.*

HEROD.
Herod the great, Lord of all I survey.
Every way I look the land is mine;
fine cities, fair villages, busy farms.
Cavalry, bowmen, men-at-arms.
All must pay allegiance to me
and more: all must be tithed and taxed,
this year as before. All that I could desire,
yet something disquiets me. I hear
strange tales, stories of odd portents,
murmurs of disaffection. Nothing to put
a finger on, nothing concrete, just
a feeling. I've sent my agents
everywhere, hunting down the rumours:
yet, so far, nothing. We must be vigilant.

During this the three KINGS *have arrived at his palace.*

1ST KING.
King Caspar of Saba.

2ND KING.
King Melchior of Tarsus.

3RD KING.
King Balthasar of Arabia.

HEROD.
Welcome, gentlemen, welcome. This is indeed
an honour: to receive not just one dignitary,

but three. Some refreshment? You seem weary,
and must have travelled far.

1ST KING.
    We have. Come by separate ways,
    following a star.

HEROD.
    A star?

2ND KING.
    A star that shines like a beacon from afar.

HEROD.
    A beacon?

3RD KING.
    We all agree it is the fulfilment
    of an ancient prophecy.

HEROD.
    A prophecy. I see.

1ST KING.
    We seek safe-conduct through your realm,
    to celebrate a Royal Birth.

2ND KING.
    A great Prince will be born under this brilliant star.

3RD KING.
    A King of Kings, to rule every nation,
    near or far.

HEROD.
    A King of Kings! A Prince of Princes!
    Gentlemen, you interest me mightily.
    Where exactly will you find this prodigy?

1ST KING.
    We don't know yet: when the star stops,
    then we believe we will find Him.

HEROD.
    Gentlemen, noble monarchs: if this comes true,
    and you do find this infant potentate, please
    do me the honour of returning here at once,
    so that I might make homage too to one so great.

1ST KING.
    Of course.

2ND KING.
> Of course.

3RD KING.
> That goes without saying.

HEROD.
> Now noble friends, I won't delay
> you any further on your mission.
> Travel where you will — I await your return
> with greatest interest — go with my blessing.
> Let's hope you'll bring the best of news.

They exit. Resume their journey round the path. JOSEPH *and*
MARY *begin to form Nativity Tableau.*

> A King of Kings! A Prince of Princes!
> King of the Jews! An infant born to rule
> the world! And where will that leave me?
> What use will all these riches be,
> if I'm subject to someone else's whims?
> I'll track Him down, dispose of Him,
> before He can do any harm. I won't alarm
> them, mustn't appear too anxious. I'll say
> I want to pay Him homage as they do. Then,
> when they've gone, I'll pay Him homage
> in a different way.

Lights out on HEROD.

SHEPHERDS *and* ANGEL *on Central Cross. The* KINGS *to
the* HOLY FAMILY.

ANGEL.
> In a stable in this small town
> God has come down to earth
> in the form of man. Who will be
> the first to greet Him? First to see
> the Saviour. Why not these three?
> Three lads from Pontefract.
> Poor shepherd lads with hardly a sheep
> between them.

1ST SHEPHERD.
> Lord, I sometimes think I'd be better off
> six feet under. No sooner decent weather

than it's thunder and lightning and rain
again.

2ND SHEPHERD.

Whenever you get ahead, a few bob in your pocket,
what happens? Prices go up like a rocket,
something always goes wrong.

1ST SHEPHERD.

This time, it's the sheep. It's enough
to make you weep. I'm off to Wakefield fair
to try and pick up a ewe or two there.

3RD SHEPHERD.

A bit of a bevvy, eh! A night on the ale?

1ST SHEPHERD.

A sale, more like. I'm going to look for sheep,
See if I can get something on the cheap.

2ND SHEPHERD.

Why is it that prices always go up and
never come down?
You could spend a fortune in that town:
I don't know where other folk get their cash.

3RD SHEPHERD.

I don't know about you two, but I'm starving.
I've had nowt since breakfast and not much at that.

2ND SHEPHERD.

My stomach thinks my throat's been cut.

3RD SHEPHERD.

What've we got? – A chicken-leg, some sausage
and a pie!
By, that looks good.

1ST SHEPHERD.

Two Bury puddings, a pig's trotter and some tripe.

2ND SHEPHERD.

The carcass from the hare we ate last night.
Put them together and we've got a feast!

They sit down, spread the food out.

3RD SHEPHERD.

I could really go a drink with this lot.

1ST SHEPHERD.
>   Well, as it so happens, I've got some ale with me
>   Homebrew, strong stuff, too. (*Drinks.*)

3RD SHEPHERD.
>   After you. (*Drinks.*) Ay, it's good stuff all right.

2ND SHEPHERD.
>   All right, all right, don't hog it.
>   Let's have a swig. By, that's strong.

3RD SHEPHERD.
>   It'll not last long if you go at it like that.
>   Give it here.

2ND SHEPHERD.
>   You might be a lousy shepherd, but you brew
>   good beer!

1ST SHEPHERD.
>   There's some as got hollow legs round here.

3RD SHEPHERD.
>   I could just do with a few minutes' kip.

>   *He belches contentedly, lies down.*

2ND SHEPHERD.
>   Ay, a few minutes' shuteye wouldn't go amiss.

>   *He lies down.*

1ST SHEPHERD (*stretching*).
>   Now that you mention it,
>   I wouldn't mind resting the eyes a bit myself.

ANGEL.
>   They've fallen asleep after a few pints of ale.
>   Soon they will wake and find life changed forever.

>   *The 'star' effect.*

>   Wake up! Wake up, you shepherd lads, and see
>   Creation's greatest mystery! In Bethlehem
>   a son is born to Him who rules all.
>   They call Him Jesus, He who is sent
>   to save us. Get up and go, pay homage
>   to your infant King, and the Virgin girl
>   who bore Him. Sing His praise,

Son of the Ancient of days.
Just follow this bright star.

Live music – possibly played by exiting ANGEL *– as they wake up.*

1ST SHEPHERD.
I dreamt an angel spoke to me!

2ND SHEPHERD.
Me too! What did he say to you?

1ST SHEPHERD.
To follow the bright star to Bethlehem,
where we'll see . . .

3RD SHEPHERD.
. . . Him who will rule over all.
Come to redeem us from the Fall,
and make us pure. It's the same dream,
I'm sure . . .

1ST SHEPHERD.
Perhaps it wasn't a dream.

2ND SHEPHERD.
Come on, we've far to go.

3RD SHEPHERD.
But what will we take for offerings?
What have we got?

1ST SHEPHERD.
Not a lot. But just take what you can.
If He's really the Son of Man, He'll understand.

2ND SHEPHERD.
He's only a nipper anyway.
I'll take Him a lamb to play with.

3RD SHEPHERD.
Good idea. Let's go. Follow that star,
the Angel said . . .

2ND SHEPHERD.
Hey, wait a minute. There was a lamb here,
brand new,
I'll swear it. The ewe dropped it last night.
Right here, it was. That's damned queer . . .

1ST SHEPHERD.

    I missed one, too, only the other day.

3RD SHEPHERD.

    They do say there's a few gone missing round here,
    lately. Happen I know where they've gone to.

2ND SHEPHERD.

    I'm thinking the same as you.

3RD SHEPHERD.

    Ay, someone as lives not so far from here.

1ST SHEPHERD.

    It's Mack we're talking about, isn't it?

2ND SHEPHERD.

    I'd put my money on it any day.

3RD SHEPHERD.

    Right. It's not so far out of our way; let's go
    there now.

1ST SHEPHERD.

    He can't have got much further, anyhow.

They cross to Keep Stage – MACK's cottage, GILL asleep.

MACK (*urgent, furtive*).

               Gill! Gill! Wake up quick!
    For God's sake, woman, where are you?

GILL.

    Who? What? Who is it?

MACK.

    Who d'you think it is? Old Nick? It's me, Mack.
    Open up, quick!

GILL (*letting him in*).

               You make me sick.
    Coming home all hours, always promises.
    Anything rather than do an honest job.

MACK.

    I've done a job, all right. But not an honest one.
    (*He produces a plump lamb from under his coat.*)
    Look! Now perhaps you can cook me a decent meal
    or two. Ay, more than a few!
    Chops, gigot, best end of neck,

breast, kidneys, shoulder . . . by heck,
we can live for weeks.
Carrots, onions, taters,
a few leeks . . .

GILL.

Come in here before someone sees you.
You'll be the death of us.
(*Grudgingly.*) It's a fine plump one, I'll say that.
Where d'you get it?

MACK.

That lot up the hill. Gib and John and that
young one.

GILL.

A bit too close for comfort. A bit too bold
if you ask me. They know you of old.
What if they come here nosing about?
We'd be through. There's three of them and only
one of you.

MACK.

That's true.
What'll we do?

GILL.

Trust you. When it's trouble it's always *we.*
All right. Leave it to me. (*Thinks.*)
I'll tell you what I'll do . . .

*She whispers in his ear. They laugh delightedly. Turn and busy
themselves. Meanwhile the* SHEPHERDS *have reached*
MACK's *cottage.*

1ST SHEPHERD.

Mack, are you there? Open up a minute.

2ND SHEPHERD.

Mack, do you hear?

MACK.

Who's there?

3RD SHEPHERD.

John and Gib and me. The three of us are off
on a journey. We thought we'd stop by and see
you, like.

MACK.
It's not very convenient.

1ST SHEPHERD.
That's not very neighbourly.

MACK.
We've got problems here.

2ND SHEPHERD.
Let us in. What else are neighbours for?

MACK.
You don't understand. It's the missus . . .

3RD SHEPHERD.
What, Gill? What's up with her? Not ill
is she? You'd best let us in to have a looksee.

1ST SHEPHERD.
I agree. You might need help.

2ND SHEPHERD.
Yes, let us in. It's freezing out here.

MACK.
Oh, very well. Just a minute.

He lets them in. GILL *in bed. In a cradle next to her is the
lamb. Wrapped up in baby clothes. It's a Nativity Tableau.*

3RD SHEPHERD.
Mack! Mack, lad, you never told us she was
expecting.

1ST SHEPHERD.
Ay, we'd not have bothered you if we'd known.

2ND SHEPHERD.
Sorry. (*Slightly suspicious still.*) A bit
premature, wasn't it?

MACK.
Well, actually, there's been complications.
She's under the doctor.

1ST SHEPHERD.
She's been under someone, that's for sure.

2ND SHEPHERD.
Well, best be off. Congratulations, love.

3RD SHEPHERD.
>Ay, all the best. What are you going to call it?

1ST SHEPHERD.
>Is it a lass or a lad?

MACK.
>Er . . . we've not named him yet. I'm ever so glad
>you called. (*Trying to shoo them out.*)
>You must come and wet the baby's head
>when you get back.

>*A distinctly sheep-like noise from the cradle.*

2ND SHEPHERD (*very suspicious now*).
>   Let's have a look at the
>little feller. (*Peers into cot.*) He looks a
>bit sheepish to me.

3RD SHEPHERD.
>Hang on, let's see . . . Hey, look at the ears
>on him!

1ST SHEPHERD.
>And that nose. God knows what he'll look like
>when he grows up.

2ND SHEPHERD.
>With a gob like that he'd sup enough.

GILL.
>I . . . I know he looks a bit odd, but he'll grow.

3RD SHEPHERD.
>I swear to God, I've never seen a baby with
>*horns* before.

1ST SHEPHERD.
>Perhaps it's the Devil's doing. He's ugly enough.
>Who d'you think he takes after?

>*An unmistakable bleat now.*

>Ar! He's crying! Perhaps he wants to be picked
>up. (*Does so.*) There, there. Your Uncle Gib will
>look after you. (*Puts it down.*) Just sit there a
>minute. Now, lads, what's to do? To celebrate
>the happy event before we go?

2ND SHEPHERD.
    I know.

*He takes a blanket from the bed. They catch on, grab MACK,
put him in the blanket and toss him in the air. GILL cowers in
bed.*

ALL.
    One! Two! Three!

Business of this. Finally they let him crash to the floor.

MACK.
    Oh, me back. I'm black and blue all over.

3RD SHEPHERD.
    Well, so long.

1ST SHEPHERD.
    See you, Mack.

2ND SHEPHERD (*picks up lamb*).
                                    I think we'll take the little
    feller for a walk.

3RD SHEPHERD.
    Fresh air will do him good. Ta-ta.

*They exit with the lamb and resume their journey to the
Tableau. Music.*

1ST SHEPHERD.
    This must be the place.

2ND SHEPHERD.
    And this must be her. Did you ever see such a
    lovely face?

3RD SHEPHERD.
    It feels like some sort of Holy place . . .

1ST SHEPHERD.
    Come on, let's go and ask to see Him.

2ND SHEPHERD.
    Mistress, though we've not come very far,
    may we come in? An angel told us to follow
    a star, and find a child who's born to save
    us all from sin.

MARY.

> Welcome. Come in, all three of you. We are
> poor people, and can offer little hospitality.
> Come and see the miracle that has chosen me to
> rear Him.

> *She shows the* CHRIST-CHILD *to them.*

GOD.

> Now I have fulfilled the ancient prophecy.
> To end as it began; A man, a woman and a tree.

CHORUS.

> A man, a woman and a tree
> Symbol of immortality
> Symbol of our humanity
> A man, a woman and a tree

> This is the tree of knowledge
> This is the tree of sin
> This is the tree of passion
> The pattern must begin

> A man, a woman and a tree
> Symbol of immortality
> The story's end will always be
> A man, a woman and a tree

Finale.

Part Two
Nativity to Judgement

Music. GOD *on his throne.*

GOD.
> I am the word. And the word was the World,
> and everything in it. And, crown of my creation
> mankind. Woman and man together
> set to live in Paradise, cast out and cursed by
> me for eating from the Tree of Life.
> Time now, perhaps, to think of forgiveness.
> I will create a son to walk among men.
> In human form, the word made flesh,
> come to redeem their ancient sin.
> A man, born of woman, but son of God.

GOD *exits.* SATAN *emerges and comes on to the Keep Stage.*

SATAN.
> Ladies and Gentlemen,
> good evening. Permit me to introduce myself:
> Lucifer, sometimes better known as Satan,
> also known as Old Nick, etc, etc.
> Welcome to our little show.
> The story of my life, actually.
> Don't take any notice of that stuff
> about a man, a woman and a tree:
> the important person in this tale
> is me. First I was a star in Heaven,
> brightest of all by far. Like a beacon
> in the night. My light dazzled them.
> I could have done the job He does, no problem.
> But something inside made me rebel;
> the next thing I knew I'd been cast down
> to Hell. A setback, admittedly.
> And how I hated those creatures He created;
> 'man' they were called. And 'woman'.
> You've no idea how He indulged them.
> But I showed Him: I whispered to Eve.
> Things were never the same again,
> in fact they went from bad to worse

(or better and better, according to your point of view),
after Cain slew his brother and was cursed
through every generation. Things got so bad,
no-one listened to Him at all. Envy, lust,
avarice, greed: all the evils flourished like bindweed.
So He drowned the lot of them in a great flood.
Then there was Abraham.
A fine test He set him. I don't know
how He keeps them on His side, I really don't.
I mean, sacrifice your eldest son?
That's a bit steep. The lad could have died.
After that came Moses – a real thorn in my side
– and his wretched tribe, saved
in the nick of time. No fault of mine.
Who could possibly foresee they'd get away
across the Red Sea?
Now I've got another ally in my war against God:
someone called Herod, King of the Jews,
or so it seems. However some other monarchs
have had strange dreams. Portents.
They've travelled for weeks to get to Bethlehem.
And some shepherds too; the same thing happened to them.
So there they are, they've followed this star
and found a woman with a child
in some ruined outhouse. She claims to be a virgin –
a likely story – and says that He's the father,
no less. Where was I? Oh yes, the baby.
Well you see, if what they say is true,
this is the blackest day of all for me.
He (*Points.*), the Son of Man
is born to set the whole of Mankind free
and liberate them from the likes of me.
King of Kings, Son of God, they say.
We'll see.
There'll be some slip-ups if I get my way.

During this the three SHEPHERDS *are frozen as parts of the
Nativity Tableau. Lights up on this as* SATAN *points.*

2ND SHEPHERD.
  Mistress, though we've not come very far,
  may we come in?

An angel told us to follow a star and find a
child who's born to save us all from sin.

MARY.
Welcome. Come in, all three of you. We are
poor people and can offer little hospitality.
Come and see the miracle that has chosen me
to rear Him.

She shows the CHRIST-CHILD *to them.*

1ST SHEPHERD (*kneels*).
Lord, we give thanks for this visitation.
I've not much to offer but this linnet.
Happen it'll sing songs for him.

2ND SHEPHERD (*kneels*).
Lord, we give thanks for this visitation.
I've brought a lamb.
Perhaps they'll grow up as companions.

3RD SHEPHERD (*kneels*).
Lord, we give thanks for this visitation.
All I could find was this ball of wool.
Perhaps the lad will play with it.

MARY.
Thank you. Thank you all. These gifts though small
mean more than pearls and rubies. He who is
my other husband will remember you.

JOSEPH.
And *this* husband thanks you, too.

Enter the three KINGS.

1ST KING.
Most beautiful of all sights. Mother, child,
serenity.

2ND KING.
We have come to see the fulfilment of an ancient
prophecy.

3RD KING.
Permit me. I am Balthasar, come from far
Arabia, following the brightest star in the sky,

to where He lies, who is prophesied to reign
over us all.

1ST KING (*kneels*).
I bring a token, an unworthy offering.
Gold, as befits a future King.

2ND KING (*kneels*).
I bring a humble gift of incense,
fit for one who will be worshipped.

3RD KING.
I bring the simplest gift of all three,
myrrh, the darkest herb, foretelling death
upon a bitter tree.

ANGEL *appears*.

ANGEL.
Good lords, you have come many weary miles
to see this miracle. Faithfully you followed
the light the Lord set before you.
Your lives will be changed forever
by this night. Go directly home. Avoid
the court of Herod. He will most certainly
try to kill this newborn child.
A tyrant does not give up a crown so easily.
Now go.

They depart. The ANGEL *goes in to the* HOLY FAMILY.

Joseph, good man and true, I am an Angel
sent you from Heaven. Now you must prove
not only a good man, but a better father.
The life of the Blessed Family depends on you.
Take your wife and her new Christ-child
away into safety. You must flee immediately.
King Herod will kill without mercy
until the child who ranks above his earthly
power is no more.

JOSEPH.
I'm sure this must be true.
I will do as you say.
Mary, my dear, we must prepare to go
away. Now, sir, you say we must leave,
but where does safety lie?

ANGEL.
>In Egypt. Where Herod's evil hand
>has no command. Prepare yourselves,
>and I will journey with you.

>*The* ANGEL *escorts them on their way. Music.*

>*Fanfare.* HEROD's *court.*

CHAMBERLAIN.
>All hail Herod, mightiest of the mighty!
>Your writ runs from sea to sea, no mountain
>towers above your jurisdiction.
>From Tuscany to Turkey,
>from India to Italy,
>Syria and Sicily,
>all men fall at your feet.
>From Egypt to Mantua,
>Saracena to Susa,
>from Norway to Normandy
>all men can see the might
>of your principality.
>From Padua to Preston . . .

HEROD.
>Yes, yes, I know all that. Get on.

CHAMBERLAIN.
>With what, sire?

HEROD.
>With what I called you for.
>I've heard all this praise before.
>What news from the soothsayers?

CHAMBERLAIN (*hesitant*).
>   My Lord, they have consulted
>many tomes, ancient volumes, cast for
>auguries . . .

HEROD.
>Yes, yes, what did they say?

CHAMBERLAIN.
>They . . . They have discovered several
>prophecies!
>'*Virgo concipiet, natumque pariet*'

A virgin girl without human desire
will bear a son, says Isaiah.
He will be called Emmanuel – 'God is with us'.
Others tell
of a boy child to be born in Bethlehem.
He will become King of the Jews and mightiest
of all. Some are of the opinion . . .

During the next speech, SATAN *appears, watches approvingly.*

HEROD.
Enough! King of the Jews!
Born in Bethlehem! What kind of news
is this? This creature grows under my nose
in Bethlehem? We'll see who reigns in Israel.

Exit CHAMBERLAIN. *Enter* CAPTAIN.

A boy-child, eh? 'Emmanuel'?
'God is with us', indeed!
Well, not for long . . .
Now listen, and listen well.
I hear tell that a princeling
has been born in secret, feigning humble birth.
Go and raise a company of your most trusted men,
and kill every male child you can find.
No exceptions, mind: the one you spare
might be the very one to usurp me.
See that it's done, and quickly.

The SOLDIER *blows a whistle. Whistles from two* SOLDIERS
at other points of the Bailey. They, and SATAN, *move to the
Central Cross, driving five* WOMEN *with babies before them.
The other* MOTHERS *assemble on Baddies' stage and follow
them where the massacre takes place.*

Mothers' Song:
CHORAL/SOLO (*spoken*).
Mothers
Mothers of Africa
Mothers of Asia
Mothers of all suffering humankind
Pray for us.
Mothers

Mothers of all murdered children
Mothers of plague victims
Mothers of the starving
Say with us
These thoughts of our dear dead
Fruits of our bodies
Torn from the branch
will always stay with us.
Mothers
Mothers of all nations
Mothers at the stations
of the cross
cry with us at our loss.

(*Sung.*)
(*Verse One*)

Mothers
Who must suffer while men fight
Mothers
Waiting through the anxious night
Mothers
Who endure their starving eyes
Mothers
Who must hear their dying cries
Mothers

(*Verse Two*)

Mothers
Who must bear the fruits of war
Mothers
Who have known it all before
Mothers
Who are waiting in the rain
Mothers
Dry your tears and start again

(*Spoken.*)

Mothers
Mothers of dead children everywhere lament
And curse the tyrant's hand
The blood of these poor innocents
Cries out throughout the land
To be remembered

(Sung.)

Mothers
Who must bear the fruits of war
Mothers
Who have known it all before
Mothers
Who are waiting in the rain
Mothers
Dry your tears and start again.

JOHN THE BAPTIST *appears on the Eden Stage and
summons the audience by tolling a bell which is hanging there.*

BAPTIST.
Listen to me! The Lord Himself
has sent me as His messenger.

VOICE.
Who are you?

BAPTIST.
In this world of wickedness, my voice
is a voice crying in the wilderness.

VOICE.
Are you the promised Messiah?

BAPTIST.
I am sent to tell you to make His path straight.
Change your ways before it is too late.

VOICE.
Have you come down to Earth amongst us?

BAPTIST.
Not I. I'm no Messiah. Just plain John,
son of Zachariah and Elizabeth.
Her niece, Mary of Nazareth
has borne a son who will come among you
as a King. I am merely here to sing
His praises; He is truly the son of God
come to live on earth. Prepare for the coming
of one whose bootlaces I'm not fit
to fasten. I, John, give you this advice:
Listen. Prepare yourselves. Think on.

An ANGEL *appears above him.* GOD *watches above them.*

ANGEL.

>John, John, soon the one you spoke of
>will be with you. Your distant cousin
>in His earthly line, and son of God,
>and cousin to us all.
>As a sign to start His ministry
>on earth, the Lord His Father sends Him to you
>for baptism.

BAPTIST.

>Baptism! I'm not worthy even to touch Him!

ANGEL.

>The Lord Commands. The decision
>is not in your hands.

BAPTIST.

>What can I say? I can only obey
>and bless the day that brings Him here.

>*Enter* JESUS *walking through audience accompanied by a*
>MUSICIAN.

JESUS.

>John, worthier servant of the Lord my Father,
>I come to meet you at His command.
>Give me your hand. I greet you
>in the name of my Mother, and bring her fondest
>wishes to yours.
>Baptise me, John, wash me in the waters
>of the River Jordan.

>*Business of his baptism.* GOD *watching from above. A bright*
>*light descends towards him, hovers above his head.*

BAPTIST.

>*In nomine patris et filii*
>*et spiritus sancti.* In the name of
>the Father, Son and Holy Ghost
>all three in one, I, John,
>baptise You.

JESUS.

>Thank you. From now on
>men will call you John the Baptist.
>Those who wish to follow must be

baptised, like me, in clear water.
Here's a gift, and a prophecy.

He gives him a woollen garment that has become a lamb.

This little creature shall be
the Lamb of God.
Like me, he will be sacrificed.
I am prophesied to end my life
on a tree.
Go, John, and tell them:
those who repent their sins will have
eternal life, through me. Baptise them
in my name, and that of my Father.
Farewell, and may He be with you.

JOHN *and* JESUS *exit severally.*

Fanfare. PILATE'S COURT *enters.* LAZARUS's *tomb is on the*
Forestage. During the ensuing scene, JESUS *is welcomed in*
dumbshow by MARTHA *and* MARY. *He raises* LAZARUS.

PILATE.
Tell me, how much of a problem is this man?
Can He really rouse the people against us?
Annas?

ANNAS.
Well, My Lord Pilate, He certainly has a large following.
A popular uprising is not out of the question.

PILATE.
So, what is your Church's view on this, Caiaphas?
Should we let it pass, or is there something more,
problems in store in the future?

CAIAPHAS.
Difficult to say. Of course the man's a
heretic, and possibly a dangerous one.

ANNAS.
A subversive, too.

CAIAPHAS.
The problem is, do we want to make a martyr of him?
He may be more of a problem dead than alive.

ANNAS.
>   True. He might well survive, posthumously.
>   These cults thrive on such things. Whereas
>   if you let him be, people might see sense, in time.

PILATE.
>   So what is your complaint, Annas?

ANNAS.
>   He's been going round apparently working miracles.
>   You know the kind of thing that excites the crowd.
>   Only the other day he made someone come back
>   from the dead.

CAIAPHAS.
>   They say.

Lights down on them. Up on Forestage.

JESUS.
>   Dear Father in Heaven, I need Your help today.
>   We pray for the Soul of Lazarus, recently dead.
>   Pour down Your blessings on his head,
>   Restore him living to his friends
>   and loving sisters, Martha and Magdalene.
>   You with whom nothing ends and everything begins
>   forgive us our sins, look kindly on this
>   departed brother.
>   In the name of my mother and myself,
>   Amen. Now Lazarus, return from that dark place
>   we all must go to. Rise, and start your life
>   anew.

LAZARUS *rises from the grave.*

LAZARUS.
>   Lord, I have been in an awful place,
>   suspended in time and space. The dark kingdom
>   that awaits us all. Prince and peasant,
>   housewife and whore, townsfolk and farmer,
>   all are sure to end there. Death,
>   the one great certainty. And you have chosen
>   to deliver me from its cold embrace.
>   I have felt its foul breath, looked upon its face.
>   Now I am free to breathe again,

to see the sky, the laughter in my sister's eyes.
What other gift half so precious as this?

Lights go down on this. Back to Main Stage.

ANNAS.

He's too proud to submit to our religious
observances:
He's broken the Sabbath, criticised the laws,
publicly sided with whores. He has profaned the
Temple, thrown out the money-changers,
smashed up their stalls.

CAIAPHAS.

Worse than all this, though,
He claims to be part of some tripartite deity:
Jehovah, The Holy Spirit, and Him, Jesus.

PILATE.

I see now what all the fuss is about.

CAIAPHAS.

And from the government's point of view,
He refuses to pay homage to you, the Romans.
Says His Father is the only one He takes orders from.

PILATE.

Sounds dangerous to me. On balance, I think,
better out of the way.

CAIAPHAS.

Precisely what I was going to say.

Enter SATAN. He murmurs a message to PILATE.

PILATE.

Well, here's an interesting development, gentlemen.
A follower of the very man. He wishes to talk to me.
Send him in.

*Enter JUDAS. Exit SOLDIER. During the next, SATAN enters,
listens.*

JUDAS.

My Lord, your Reverence, my humble greetings.
I hope I don't interrupt your meeting; but if
I may make so bold, I think I could be of use to you —
if what I've been told is true.

PILATE.

> Very well. What is this favour you propose to
> bestow on us?

JUDAS.

> Both Government and Church are worried by Jesus
> the Nazarene; there's been rumour, talk. They
> think I am one of His followers; disciples,
> as He calls them. I admit I was taken in at
> first. He has charisma, beyond a doubt.
> But now I want to get out, and I want what's due
> to me.

PILATE.

> You begin to interest me. Tell me more; what's
> your name?

JUDAS.

> Judas, Sir, Judas Iscariot. Well, in brief,
> He says throw up your lot in life and follow me.
> Give all away to the poor. Well, I mean to say,
> I had investments, a little bit put by.
> But, no, it all had to go. And a woman came
> only the other day, saying she'd been no better
> than she should be, but now He's made her see
> the error of her ways.
> Brought incredibly costly oils and creams: sort
> of things a woman dreams about. He let her
> cover Him in them, bathe His feet.
> It was like washing in money. We could have
> sold them and made a fortune between us.
> I said so but would He listen? No.
> So there you are, Sir. I'm broke.
> Frankly, it's no joke.

CAIAPHAS.

> So what exactly do you propose?

JUDAS.

> I'm privy to His plans. I can make sure you'll
> be there when He's unaware. Leave it to me.
> I'll deliver Him into your hands, you'll see.

ANNAS.

> And your price?

JUDAS.
> Very reasonable. Taking everything into
> consideration, I reckon I'm owed, say,
> thirty silver pieces.

PILATE.
> I don't foresee any difficulty with that. Do
> you agree, Gentlemen? Done. It is, as they say, a deal.

They deal the money out to him. SATAN *exuberant.*

JESUS *preparing for the last supper on the Keep Stage.*

JESUS.
> Through the Grace of the Lord my Father
> eat and drink me for the last time.
> Taste this good bread and wine.

He passes the bread and wine round the table.

> Before the day is out, one of you will betray me
> you'll see. The betrayer will be the one
> who shares a plate with me.

Enter JUDAS.

JUDAS.
> I'm sorry I'm late, Lord. I was held up.
> Gosh, I'm thirsty. Lord, may I share your cup?

He drinks, then takes a piece of bread from JESUS's *plate, dips
it in the wine, eats.*

JESUS.
> Judas, you are welcome. Now I will repeat:
> one of you who eat with me tonight will betray me.

Chorus of protest, 'Not me', etc.

PETER.
> Lord, I would never betray You.

JESUS.
> Perhaps not. Who can say? But before today
> is out you will deny me three times
> to my enemies.

PETER.
> No, Lord, no.

JESUS.
> It must be so.

> JESUS *then washes the feet of his* DISCIPLES. *A voice is heard singing (wordlessly) the song we will hear later over* DOUBTING THOMAS.

> Now we have drunk and ate
> come with me to Olivet, to pray.
> I mean to stay the night,
> prepare myself until first light.
> Come.

> GOD *appears on the Keep. He speaks, but not directly to* JESUS, *who is still praying.*

> Son, Son,
> like a fledgling from the nest
> You're on Your own. Do Your best
> to bear the coming suffering.
> Soon You will reign in Heaven
> on the right hand of my throne.
> I can't help You now, You're human
> and humankind must face its death
> alone.

Interval.

Music. JESUS *and* DISCIPLES *enter and take up positions on the keep,* JESUS *praying, the others asleep as a* BOY'S VOICE *sings.*

BOY'S VOICE.
>Father, Father
>Why have You forsaken me?
>Please don't leave me
>Here among my enemies
>One touch of Your hand
>And You could set me free
>Father, Father
>Why have You forsaken me?
>
>Father, Father
>Why have You forsaken me?
>Please don't leave me
>In despair and misery
>If You love Your Son
>Then come and comfort me
>Father, Father
>Why have You forsaken me?

PILATE, JUDAS, SATAN *and* SOLDIERS *enter from Motte left carrying torches.*

PILATE.
>Now, Judas, go and earn your fee;
>show me this malcontent who plagues
>the priesthood so.

JUDAS.
>Sir, arrest Him who I go to kiss.
>Don't miss Him. His followers may
>try to help Him get away.

JUDAS *goes over to* JESUS, *embraces him.*

JUDAS.
>Lord, it's good to see you. How come
>You're still awake?

JESUS.
>I was awaiting you. Judas, you overplay
>your part, as always.

SOLDIER.
>Jesus of Nazareth?

JESUS.
>   Yes.

SOLDIER.
>   I arrest You for conspiring and plotting against
>   the State.

PETER.
>   Never!

He cuts off the SOLDIER's *ear with a blow of his sword.*

JESUS.
>   Peter, Peter, it's too late.
>   Violence is no solution.
>   Here friend, let me see.

He replaces the severed ear. It heals.

SOLDIER.
>   I . . . It . . . It's healed! My ear!
>   There's no blood, no pain,
>   I'm all in one piece again!

PILATE.
>   Come, let's have done with all this.
>   Let's hand him over to the priests, and let them
>   deal with it. This is a messy business
>   I see no good coming of it.

JESUS *is handed over to the two* TORTURERS. ANNAS *and*
CAIAPHAS, *accompanied by* FLUNKIES *carrying seats, go to
the Cross. The* TORTURERS *drag and beat* JESUS *to the
Cross.* PETER *shadows this progress.*

1ST TORTURER.
>   Hey, hup! Giddup there!

2ND TORTURER.
>   Come on, sunshine, you'll be late for your appointment.
>   My lord Caiaphas doesn't like to be kept waiting.

1ST TORTURER (*pushing him*).
>   Now see what you've done.
>   You want to watch where you're going.

2ND TORTURER.
>   Don't want to fall down the Palace steps, do we?

JESUS *falls at* CAIAPHAS's *feet.* PETER *in front row of audience.*

CAIAPHAS.
Is this all? The full extent of your haul?

1ST TORTURER.
Yes, sir. The others scarpered. You should have seen them go.

2ND TORTURER.
They didn't want to know about him.
Three times, I asked one of them:
'Do you know this man?'

PETER.
No, not me.

2ND TORTURER.
Isn't he your leader? Jesus of Nazareth?

PETER.
Never heard of him.

1ST TORTURER.
I'm sure I've seen you with him.

PETER.
I've never seen him before.

1ST TORTURER.
Anyway, we've got the ringleader here, sir.
Sullen sort, too. Not a word out of him.

CAIAPHAS.
Now listen to me, and get this into Your head:
just loosen Your tongue, or it'll be the worse
for You. My friends here might loosen a tooth
or two instead. A belt round the head might
wake You up. So let's hear from You:
who knows, it might make them better disposed
towards You.

ANNAS.
Et omnis qui tacet hic consentir videtur.
I'm sure you understand?

CAIAPHAS.
Now, what's all this about being a king?
I've heard people sing Your praises as the new Messiah.

ANNAS.

> Don't say You didn't say so. There's no smoke
> without fire. Now look,
> My friend Caiaphas and I are reasonable men –
> not kings, admittedly, but Prelates, men
> of substance – and in Your circumstances
> I'd advise a full statement, admitting guilt,
> asking for circumstances to be taken into consideration.
> Make a clean breast of it. Treason against the
> Nation, but unintentional, perhaps . . .

CAIAPHAS.

> Leave it to these chaps here. There's only one
> language they understand. You need a heavy hand.

ANNAS.

> Now, now, we don't want trouble if we can avoid it.
> No use getting annoyed. Better all round.
> *Et hoc nos volumus, quod de jure possumus*, you
> know . . . Now, we've heard these rumours
> about You claiming to be the Son of God. Surely
> these reports must exaggerate?

JESUS.

> I AM THE SON OF GOD!
> Though you may think I die
> I shall return from on high
> riding on clouds of glory!

CAIAPHAS.

> The Son of God? A likely story!
> This rag-arsed clod? I think we should
> finish him off.

ANNAS.

> Not now! *Sed nobis non licet*
> *interficere quemquam.* As the statutes say,
> the law must take its course, don't forget.

CAIAPHAS.

> Very well, let's leave him to those two
> to soften him up.

> *Exit* CAIAPHAS *and* ANNAS.

1ST TORTURER.

> Now then, You look tired. You need a rest.
> Let's fetch You a buffet. (*Hits him.*)

2ND TORTURER.
Yes, that's it, a nice buffet. (*Hits him.*)

1ST TORTURER (*dragging him to his knees*).
Now then,
how about a little game to pass the time away?

He blindfolds him.

1ST TORTURER.
We'll call it: 'Blind Man's Buffet'.
Now . . . Guess who? (*Hits him.*)

2ND TORTURER.
Yes . . . Guess who? (*Hits him.*)

*They dance around him, as in Blind Man's Buff, laughing,
hitting him as they go. He ends up in a heap on the floor.*

1ST TORTURER (*breathless*).
There, that was fun, wasn't it?

2ND TORTURER (*also breathless*).
A game fit for a king.

Enter CAIAPHAS *and* ANNAS.

CAIAPHAS.
Well, gentlemen, we've had our fun.
Now I think His problems have begun
in earnest.

ANNAS.
Take Him to Pilate. We feel it more appropriate
that He be tried by the State.

CAIAPHAS.
We certainly don't want to mix
the Church with politics.

They drag him to confront PILATE.

PILATE.
Now look here. I'm not a difficult man. I am
not unmerciful. I have certain prerogatives.
I could give You freedom: one word, and You
will live. It's well within my gift. But You
must acknowledge my jurisdiction over You.

JESUS.
>You have jurisdiction, true. But there is one
>that has jurisdiction over you, and that is God,
>my Father.
>Treat me as you will, His will shall prevail
>when you quail before Him on Judgement Day.

PILATE.
>Well, well. A proud one, eh? Truculent, I'd say.
>Still, never let it be said I wasn't fair. We
>have a law: the people may choose a felon to be released.
>What do you say?

1ST TORTURER.
>Give us Barabbas!

2ND TORTURER.
>I'd choose Barabbas any day.

PILATE.
>Very well, you've had your say.
>Now take Him away.
>Take him to Golgotha, the place of execution.
>The crucifix, of course. The standard
>punishment for heretics.
>I fear this day will prove a black one.
>However, the law must take its course.
>I wash my hands of this business forthwith.

2ND TORTURER.
>Now, my proud king, let's see
>what a bit of scourging can do
>to knock a little humility into You.

>*They strip him, tie him to a post, lash him. When he's
>unconscious, they untie him. He drops to the floor. They haul
>him to his feet.*

1ST TORTURER.
>Now, let's see . . . Yes, here it is.
>Since You're our King, You ought to have
>something to symbolise Your office.

2ND TORTURER.
>So here's a crown we've made for You.
>Rough and ready, perhaps, but it's the thought
>that counts.

They cram the crown of thorns on his head.

That's better. Now here's a little job for You:
pick up that cross and carry it through
the town. It's quite light, You'll see.

1ST TORTURER.
  And don't drop it, mind:
  it's government property.

  JESUS *drags his cross along the duckboards, through the
  crowd, stumbling and falling.* PILATE *and* SATAN *follow.*
  MARY *and* MARY MAGDALENE *are in the crowd. He
  reaches them at the Central Cross.*

MARY.
  Son, son, what have they brought You to?
  Why must they do this awful thing to You
  of all men?

JESUS.
  Mother, it is only I of all men
  who must suffer this. Only I can bear
  this bitter cross. Try and bear
  the dreadful loss.

MARY MAGDALENE.
  Lord, I can't bear to see
  them do this to You. Why must they
  treat You so?

JESUS.
  Sister, they know no better.
  I love you dearly. I will see
  Mother and you again within
  three days.

1ST TORTURER.
  And about time too. Hanging about
  rabbiting on to whingeing women.
  D'You think we've nothing better to do?

  JESUS *picks up the cross, staggers on to near the Keep Stage,
  then falls.*

2ND TORTURER.
  Oh, gawd, that's all we need.
  He's flaked out on us.

He sees SIMON OF CYRENE.

Hey, you!
Take this, and help this poor sod
hump it up the hill.

SIMON.
Sire, I'm here on business. I've an appointment
very soon. At noon, in fact. I'd like
to help this poor chap, he's in an awful state
but, really, I'm already late . . .

1ST TORTURER.
You'll be later still if you cool your heels
in the Bridewell. Do I have to tell you twice?

2ND TORTURER.
Anyway, noon, you said. None
too soon. He'll be brown bread
by then.

SIMON.
I can't stand by and see Him die
alone like this. Come on, friend,
whoever You are. I'll give You a lift.

*They carry the cross together up over the Keep Stage to the
platform at the foot of the Keep. Exit* SIMON. *The*
TORTURERS *lay the cross down.*

1ST TORTURER.
Right. Let's get on. Any last words?
Like to say a few?

JESUS.
Father, forgive them, for they know not
what they do.

2ND TORTURER.
Oh, I forgot. He's King of the Jews.

1ST TORTURER.
Now then, Your Majesty, let's see
what we can do for You. If You'd care
to just recline . . .

They throw him down onto the cross, spread his arms.

. . . that's fine.

2ND TORTURER.
Now then, let's get You nice and secure.

They tie him to the cross.

1ST TORTURER.
Here's a couple of trusty nails. The method
never fails.

2ND TORTURER.
Now, Your Majesty the King: just grit Your teeth
You won't feel a thing.

They nail him to the cross. Other SOLDIERS *come around to help.*

Now . . . One, two, three and . . .
up we go! . . .

With great exertion they haul it upright. JESUS *in agony. A* BOY'S VOICE *sings.*

BOY'S VOICE.
Father, Father
Why have You forsaken me?
Please don't leave me
Dying on this awful tree
One touch of Your hand
Could take this pain from me
Father, Father
Why have You forsaken me?

Father, Father
Why have You forsaken me?
Please don't leave me
Hanging here in agony
If You love Your Son
Then come and rescue me
Father, Father
Why have You forsaken me?

JESUS.
Father . . . Forgive them . . . They don't know what
they do!

1ST TORTURER.
Oh yes we do. You're only the latest
of quite a few.

2ND TORTURER.
>   And not the last.

>   *A peal of thunder.*

JESUS.
>   The light dies in my eyes.
>   The die is cast.
>   ELOI, ELOI, LAMA SABATHANAY!
>   Father, Father why have You forsaken me?

>   *He is dead.* MARY *and a* CHORUS OF WOMEN *sing* Stabat
>   Mater.

CHORUS.
>   *Stabat mater dolorosa*
>   *Juxta crucem lacrimosa*
>   *Dum pendebat Filius.*

MARY.
>   How much grief can a woman bear?
>   How much pain can a mother share
>   With her own son hanging there?

>   How can she bear the awful loss?
>   How can she contemplate the cross
>   Where He dies in agony?

>   How can I stand by and see
>   My only son depart from me
>   Fastened to this dreadful tree?

>   And why the fearful sacrifice
>   He must make to pay the price
>   That saves us all from sin?
>   Let it begin.

(Spoken.)
>   He will be crowned in Heaven.
>   King of all but Him who made Him in me.
>   Soon He will be free.

(Sung.)
>   Lord, let the next one be me.

CHORUS.
>   *Quanduo corpus morietur*
>   *Fac et animae donetur*
>   *Paradisi gloria.*
>   Amen.

1ST TORTURER.

> Well, that's it. The end of another one.

2ND TORTURER.

> What about His clobber? They might fetch
> a bob or two . . .

The TORTURERS *begin to lower* JESUS *from the cross. Music: Dies Irae. The* DISCIPLES *lift* JESUS *from the cross and carry him tenderly to the tomb on Eden Stage. They are accompanied by* GUARDS *who seal up the door of the tomb. The disembodied* VOICE OF GOD *is heard.*

GOD.

> The ending of our tale shall be
> a man, a woman and a tree.
> Now from human form set free
> down to Limbo he must go
> to challenge Satan's mastery.

Drumming from the Central Cross. SATAN *is standing there hammering a pole on the cross while three other* DEVILS *accompany him and four others dance wildly. At the end of this they rush towards the Baddies' Stage where the shadow play has been set up.*

Light out on GOD. *We see a shadow play of the following with voices over. They are all in Limbo.*

ADAM.

> Stuck here since time began
> because my disobedience
> led to the fall of man.

EVE.

> Adam, love, don't blame yourself
> forever more. You've paid for it
> a thousandfold, and more.

ADAM.

> And yet I see a distant light
> beyond this awful place.

ISAIAH.

> You're right. I see a face
> that shines through this eternal gloom,
> this shadow world beyond the tomb.

SIMEON.
>You're right. I know that face. Another time,
>another place. The Roman hyacinths were
>blooming in bowls. I, Simeon, weary and old
>was privileged to see Him who will reign
>for all eternity.

BAPTIST.
>After this purgatory, we will be set free,
>set free by Him whom I baptised
>to start His ministry.

MOSES.
>This is the hour I
>prophesied. Now Satan's reign
>will be denied.

1ST DEVIL.
>Denied? My master? He rules
>forever where you wait in torment
>until he decides your fate.

2ND DEVIL.
>True, the air seems brighter here,
>a clear light shines where there was none
>before. We can't ignore this threat.
>Come, Belial and Balith, Ashtaroth
>and Lilith! We will conquer yet!

SATAN.
>I reign forever! And forever more!
>What rash intruder ventures to Hell's door?

JESUS.
>*Attolite portas, principes, vestas et elevamini*
>*portae aeternales, et introbit rex gloriae!*
>Out, demons, out, I say!

1ST DEVIL.
>Good Lord Satan, save us!
>I feel like a toad beneath the harrow.
>Blackest fear chills me to the marrow!

SATAN.
>No mere mortal could do
>what you're attempting to – I know you.
>Son of a carpenter and Mary of Nazareth.

You breathed your last breath
some hours ago on Calvary.

JESUS.

But now see the power of Him
who is my Father in Heaven
who cast you, Lucifer, and your seven
rebel angels out from bliss,
into this black abyss.
Now I, *Christus Pantocrator*
will drive you and your friends before me
to harrow you down to Hell!

Dies Irae. Screams and howls as SATAN *and* DEVILS *are cast into Hell.*

JESUS.

Now, Adam and sister Eve, Moses, Isaiah
leave this awful Limbo. Simeon
and brother Baptist, go into brightest Heaven,
where my Father waits for you in Glory.

A commotion by the entrance of the Castle. A CENTURION
and three SOLDIERS *force their way roughly and noisily
through the crowd, ending at the Baddies' Stage where*
PILATE *is waiting.*

CENTURION.

My Lord Pilate, this town abounds
with rumours. Portents, strange sounds.
The sun at noon black as midnight.
Graves have opened up. These sights,
they say, have only been seen
since the execution of the Nazarene.

PILATE.

Mere idle tales. Superstitions.

CENTURION.

I agree, Sir. The merest superstitions.
And yet . . .

PILATE.

What? Out with it!

CENTURION.

This . . . troublemaker, rabble rouser,
call Him what you may, was heard to say

> to His so-called disciples that He
> would rise again and join them
> after three days. And today's . . .

PILATE.
> Day three. I see.
> The last thing we want is that sort of rumour
> spreading. Who knows what sort of thing
> we may be heading for. No, we'll scotch it,
> now. Get over to that tomb and guard it well.
> No demonstrations, no protests. Tell them
> to be on their way, or else.

SOLDIERS *to tomb on Eden Stage.*

CENTURION.
> Now, lads, I want you to look sharp,
> and keep your eyes peeled. I've got
> a feeling something's going to happen here
> tonight. And if I'm right you'll need
> your wits about you. Now, stand to.
> Arrest anything that moves.

*They mount guard. An ANGEL appears, plays music. They are
seized with a sudden sleepiness. As they succumb, a light
appears inside the tomb, the walls of which vanish. Out steps
JESUS transfigured with light.*

JESUS.
> I am returned from darkest shades
> within three days as promised.
> From henceforth this day will be made sacred
> to honour my return. Flesh made flesh again
> after a sojourn in shadow land.
> This wound, these injured hands
> and feet the emblems of my immortality.
> Those who believe in me shall live forever,
> as I do. Those who eat bread and drink wine
> in my remembrance will receive me. The flesh,
> the blood will be mine. Flesh made flesh again,
> fresh proof of our domination over death.

Light out on him. He exits. The SOLDIERS begin to wake up.

SOLDIERS.
>Sir! Sir! Wake up! Something's happened.
>Someone's sprung the tomb!

CENTURION.
>What? Let me see! Good Heavens, it's true!
>No-one could have done that alone.
>Look around, quick now!

They search to no avail.

CENTURION.
>Oh, well, that's it, blast it. Back to town;
>best to face the music right away. The Lord
>knows what Pilate's going to say.

Exit SOLDIERS.

Stabat Mater *music is heard as* SOLDIERS *exit. The three* MARYS *enter Motte right, carrying torches. They walk down over the Keep Stage, along the path and pause at the edge of the Eden Stage.*

MARY.
>Leave me here, sisters, go home.
>I'll bear my grief alone.

MARY MAGDALENE.
>No, we'll stay with you,
>and pray. But what's this?
>Didn't we seal the door? It's not like
>it was before. Why is that great lock
>thrown to the floor?

MARY (*she looks inside*).
>It's . . . It's empty!
>. . . He's, He's gone!

MARY MAGDALENE.
>Within three days, He said. I wonder . . .

MARY.
>Who could have moved Him? Why?
>Leave me, let me stay here and pray.

MARY MAGDALENE.
>Come, sister, let's go away
>and leave her. Good news
>may yet come her way.

They exit. Enter JESUS, *cloaked and hooded. She becomes aware she is being watched.*

MARY.
>Oh, you quite startled me. You came up
>so quietly. Tell me, good gardener,
>what do You know? Did You see
>what happened to the body that lay
>within this tomb?

JESUS.
>I'm sorry, Ma'am, I'm just
>a humble gardener come back
>to tend his plants, and water them with
>kindness.

MARY.
>Oh, is there no-one can say
>what happened to the body of my son?

JESUS.
>There is one, and not too far away . . .

MARY (*looks around*).
>   There's no-one . . .

JESUS *throws back his hood. Bright light on his face.*

JESUS.
>Mother, mother, do you mean to say
>you don't recognise your only son
>after three days?
>Well, I'm amazed.

His little joke is too much for her. She collapses, sobbing, clutching his hand.

MARY.
>Son, Son, if You only knew
>how much I've missed You.
>And here You are, as good as new!

JESUS.
>Not quite as new. These wounds, these weals
>upon my back will never heal. My blood
>seals the contract that absolves you all.
>Come on, Mother, no more tears. I'm only here

for a short time, then I must go and join my Father.
Mother, believe in me . . .

Both exit.

The Keep Stage. The DISCIPLES *are arriving, greeting one another.*

LUKE.
This is a desperate time. This awful crime
must not deflect us from our work. We must not
shirk the task of going on without Him.

CLEOPHAS.
True. And yet we are a team without a leader.
We need a sign, something to renew the faith
we had when He was with us. Desperate times,
indeed.

LUKE.
Agreed. Will we ever be the same again?

Enter MARY MAGDALENE *with* PETER *and* PAUL.

MARY MAGDALENE.
It's true, I tell you. There He was,
alive as you or me. You'll see.
Do you think His own mother wouldn't know Him?

PETER.
I don't know what to think. Here, give us
a drink. Oh, if only it was true. It's not
that I don't believe you, it's just that even
He . . .

PAUL.
I know what you mean, Peter. Like you I believe
He could do anything. But come back
from the grave itself?
And yet, we must believe . . .

MARY MAGDALENE.
Don't deceive yourselves. Of course, it's true.
I wouldn't tell you a lie. If you'd seen the
look in His mother's eyes!

During the above, JESUS *is seen walking slowly from Motte left, carrying a lantern. He steps down onto the Keep Stage behind the* DISCIPLES. *They have not seen him arrive. He is now in the central position in the tableau as for the Last Supper.*

JESUS.
> Well met, friends. I'm glad you started without
> me.
> Now let's see . . . where shall I sit?
> Come on, sit down, there's plenty of places.
> Lovely to see your familiar faces again.
> Come on, let's eat . . .

He distributes bread and wine, re-enacting the Last Supper.

> Eat this in the remembrance of someone
> you once knew. And drink this good wine,
> too.

DISCIPLE.
> Is it true? . . . Lord, is it really You?

JESUS.
> Excuse me, good Brothers and Sister.
> I must speak to my Father, alone.

He exits. Enter THOMAS.

MARY MAGDALENE.
> Thomas, guess what? He's returned,
> just like He said He would!

PETER.
> Isn't that good news? He's sat and broken bread
> in this very room!

MARY MAGDALENE.
> His mother saw Him first, just by the tomb . . .

THOMAS.
> Hold on. Hold on for a moment.
> Are you trying to tell me this is a real,
> flesh and blood person you've seen?

JESUS *comes in quietly during the next, and stands behind him, listening.*

> Not a ghost, or a spirit or something
> in between? Our Master came back
> in the actual flesh? I can't conceive it.

I'd like to believe it: it's probably an hallucination,
a product of your imagination. After all,
we've been through a lot lately.

JESUS.

Thomas, they were right. It *is* me.
See, here are the wounds, still fresh.
This is living flesh. You don't believe?
Then touch me.

He takes THOMAS's *hand, puts it in to the wound in his side.
It comes away covered in blood. As* THOMAS *speaks, we
hear a voice singing.*

THOMAS.

Mercy, Jesus . . . Forgive me . . .

VOICE.

Mercy, Jesus, forgive me
I was blind and couldn't see
Mercy, Jesus, forgive my doubts
Now they are all cast out
Mercy Jesus, forgive my sins
Today a new life begins.

Light up on GOD *on the Keep. A rainbow unfurls from his
feet. During this speech* JESUS *and the* DISCIPLES *move up to
the Motte, where they are joined by the whole company.*

GOD.

Now it's time for my Son to come home
and reign with me in Heaven.
His earthly ministry is over.
For forty days they have been with Him,
seen Him work further wonders,
proof enough for anyone. Now
they must understand that they
must carry on alone, when He
has come to join me on this Throne.
In my end is my beginning. Alpha
and Omega. My word
the last word: A man,
a woman and a tree.
Now the word made flesh
will come to live

with me. Born of woman,
slain by man, died
upon a tree. Now I summon Him
to reign with me in Heaven.
Seven bright angels
shall bear Him to my side.

JESUS.
Matthew, Mark, Luke, John
I look to you to carry on
without me. Peter, you
are the rock on which my church
will grow. Mary, I must go
to where my Father waits:
I'll be ready at the gates when
you come to join me. Now Mother,
no more tears. Let's see a smile
on your face. Soon you'll be with me
in a brighter place.

                              Brothers,
fellow-workers, farewell.
Words can't tell how sad I am
to leave you once again;
But I must go to where my Father waits
alone. I must sit
at the right hand of His throne.

Music. ANGELS *descend. They give him a fire dove. The
company sing the Tree Song as* JESUS *ascends to his* FATHER.
*By the end of the song, the rest of the cast are assembled on
the Keep. The* SAVED *ascend. The* DAMNED *are cast down.*

In my end is my beginning. I died
to save mankind from sinning.
Those who do not heed me will be
cast into the lower depths of Hell.
Those who do will dwell with me
in Heaven. And will be there
for all eternity. My blood
will reprieve all who believe in me.
Now Sacred Trinity, one and three
indivisible, I come to You in glory.

Goes to GOD's *right hand.*

All must believe me.
Now Father, receive me!

All the cast sing.

CHORUS.
Joy and resurrection
End to mortal strife
A triumph over Evil
Bringing everlasting life.

MARY.
Here is the crown of His passion
Here is the flower of His pain
Now is an end to sorrow
Only my love remains.

PETER.
Now He ascends to Heaven
To sit by His Father's side
All who believe will follow
Sinners renounce their pride.

CHORUS.
Joy and resurrection
End to mortal strife
A triumph over Evil
Bringing everlasting life.

QUARTET.
Heaven's gate waits before us
So do the depths of Hell
What kind of fate awaits you?
Only you alone can tell.

CHORUS.
Joy and resurrection
End to mortal strife
A triumph over Evil
Bringing everlasting life.

Fireworks. A dove of fire above their heads.

Alternative Dialogues

The following dialogues can be substituted for the Cain/Garcio episodes of Part One as marked by asterisks in the main text, in which Garcio is played as a boy and Cain drives a team of horses.

Beginning where marked on p. 14:

GARCIO.

> Hello! Hello! Hello!
> I'm Garcio. Gather round, listen and see,
> Jack the Lad, game for a laugh,
> that's me. Now settle down,
> and pin back your lugholes:
> and if you keep on chattering
> You can kiss me arsehole!

He displays his bottom to the audience.

> Thank you!
> My master, Cain, is a right good farmer,
> and I'm his right-hand man
> (he even pays me when he can).
> Here he comes right now,
> having problems with his trusty plough;
> I'm off. I've got better things to do
> than talk to you.

Exit GARCIO. *Enter* CAIN *with a plough drawn by horses and oxen.*

CAIN.

> Get up! Get up there, Greyhorn!
> Come on, Grime, Mop! Bugger me,
> I've never seen such a hopeless lot,
> they're rooted to the spot. Down,
> come on now, pull your weight,
> If you don't buck up it's the knackers' yard
> for you, mate. Donning, you idle mare,
> don't just stand there. Pull, damn you!
> Stone me!

He looks round in exasperation.

Where are you, pikehand? Have I got to do everything
on my own?

GARCIO (*aside as he appears*).
God's curse on folk who do nowt
but moan.

CAIN.
Have I to do it all myself? Didn't you hear me shout?

GARCIO.
You're always shouting. All right,
let's get them turned about.
Come on, Whitehorn, come on, Spot.
Get your arse in gear you idle lot!
(*Aside.*) They'd do better if he fed them from time to time.

CAIN.
I heard that line.
Just watch it, buggerlugs!

He slaps him. GARCIO *slaps him back.*

GARCIO.
And you watch it, too!

CAIN (*taken aback*).
Listen, I'm the boss, don't forget.

GARCIO.
And I'm the lad who gives as good as he gets.

CAIN.
All right, all right, let's get on.

Ending where marked on p. 15.

Beginning where marked on p. 19:

CAIN.
Very well, I'm cursed. So be it.
I'll keep myself to myself.
Where's that useless lad, God rot him!
Garcio! Where are you, Scumbag?

Enter GARCIO. CAIN *cuffs him about the ears.*

Come here while I hit you, scallywag!
What do you mean by it? You're never here when
you're wanted.

There's work to do.

A pit to be dug.

GARCIO.
A pit? Dug here?

CAIN.
Didn't I make myself clear?

GARCIO (*seeing the body*).
B-But it's y-your brother Abel, dead!

CAIN.
Well said. How truly observant of you.
Now, get digging.

GARCIO.
But . . . but I'm just your boy,
your servant. I'm not implicated. What
will happen if they find him? They'll blame
me too, as well as you.

CAIN.
Oh, for God's sake. All right.
If it'll keep you quiet I'll proclaim
your innocence for all to hear.
Go on, introduce me.

GARCIO.
Oyez, Oyez, Oyez!
Hear ye, Hear ye, Hear ye!

CAIN.
I solemnly proclaim . . .

GARCIO (*mocking him*).
I'm a villain. Cain's the name . . .

CAIN.
. . . That this man you know as Garcio . . .

GARCIO.
. . . a handsome lad as you well know . . .

CAIN.
. . . is innocent of any crime,
now or before . . .

GARCIO.
> ... *He's* done enough to hang himself,
> and more ...

CAIN.
> ... is innocent of any sin.

GARCIO.
> ... it's *him* who's done his brother in.

CAIN.
> There!

GARCIO (*mocking*).
> > There!

CAIN.
> Now, enough of this tomfoolery.
> Let's see you shift this plough. Go on,
> get off with you.

GARCIO.
> Goodbye one and all. I've got to go.
> God's blessing from your good friend Garcio!

Exit GARCIO. *As* CAIN *says the next he is led away by* SATAN.

Ending where marked on p. 20.

Songs

The sheet music for all the songs used in **The Wakefield Mysteries** can be obtained by writing to the composer, Andy Roberts, at the address on p. iv.

Greed and Disobedience

CHORUS.

Greed and Disobedience
Envy, Pride and Sin
A never changing pattern
See another piece begin

Lucifer the bright angel
Committed the sin of pride
Cast like a leper from heaven
With nowhere left to hide   (*Chorus.*)

Adam and Eve in the garden
Tasted forbidden fruit
Now they are banned for ever
Naked and destitute   (*Chorus.*)

Cain was jealous of Abel
Slew him on the dark hill
Committed the world's first murder
The killing continues still   (*Chorus.*)

Herod was told of Jesus
The child who will rule alone
He murdered all the small children
To preserve his earthly throne   (*Chorus.*)

Christ was betrayed by Judas
And they nailed him to a cross
Last piece of the tragic pattern
Emblem of all our loss   (*Chorus.*)

Dies Irae

> *Dies irae, dies illa*
> *Solvet saeclum in favilla:*
> *Teste David cum Sibylla.*

> Day of Wrath O day of mourning
> See fulfilled the dreadful warning
> Heav'n and earth in ashes burning.

> *Mors stupebit et natura*
> *Cum resurget creatura*
> *Judicanti responsura.*

> Worthless are your prayers and sighing
> Hear us, Lord, your grace supplying
> Rescue me from fires undying.

> *Lacrimosa dies illa*
> *Qua resurget ex favilla.*

> Man for judgement must prepare him;
> Spare, O God, in mercy spare him.

A Man, A Woman and A Tree

> A man, a woman and a tree
> Symbol of immortality
> Symbol of our humanity
> A man, a woman and a tree

> This is the tree of knowledge
> This is the tree of sin
> This is the tree of passion
> The pattern must begin

> A man, a woman and a tree
> Symbol of immortality
> The story's end will always be
> A man, a woman and a tree

Animals'/Children's Song

Seven days and seven nights,
Never stopping, day or night.
Rain till the rivers join the sea,
Covering up the tallest tree;
Rain till all the valleys fill,
Covering up the highest hill.
Seven days and seven nights
Never stopping, day or night.

Forty days and forty nights,
Sailing on by day and night.
This small family in a boat,
The only living thing afloat;
Water, water everywhere,
The only creatures God has spared.
Forty days and forty nights,
Sailing on by day and night.

Weeks and months without a stop,
Waiting till the waters drop.
Send a dove to look for land,
Now she's back on Noah's hand.
Here's her prize: a tiny leaf
Taken from an olive tree.
Weeks and months without a stop;
Suddenly, the waters drop.

While the Earth Remains
ALL.

> While the Earth remains
> Seedtime and harvest,
> Cold and heat
> Summer and winter
> And day and night
> Shall not cease.
>
> While we live in peace
> Seedtime and harvest
> Cold and heat
> Summer and winter
> And day and night
> All things will live
>
> While God forgives
> Seedtime and harvest
> Cold and heat
> Summer and winter
> And day and night
> Shall not cease

Isaac's Song

> Father, Father
> Why have you forsaken me?
> Please don't leave me
> Here to wait in agony
> One touch of your hand
> And you could set me free
> Father, Father
> Why have you forsaken me?
>
> Father, Father
> Why have you forsaken me?
> Please don't leave me
> Lying here in misery
> If you love your son
> Then take the knife from me
> Father, Father
> Why have you forsaken me?

Go Down Moses

When Israel was in Egypt's land,
Let my people go!
Oppressed so hard they could not stand,
Let my people go!
Go down, Moses,
Way down in Egypt's land,
Tell ol' Pharoah,
Let my people go!

Thus spake the Lord, bold Moses said,
Let my people go!
If not, I'll strike your first-born dead,
Let my people go!
Go down, Moses,
Way down in Egypt's land,
Tell ol' Pharoah,
Let my people go!

Ol' Pharoah thought he had us fast,
Let my people go!
But we broke his chains at last,
Let my people go!
Go down, Moses,
Way down in Egypt's land,
Tell ol' Pharoah,
Let my people go!

Magnificat

MARY.

My soul magnifies the Lord
For He has chosen me, lowest of the lowly,
and now all generations will bless me:
my spirit rejoices in God my Saviour.

My soul magnifies the Lord
He has shown great strength, He has shown great mercy,
turned away the rich and fed the needy:
my spirit rejoices in God my Saviour.

My soul magnifies the Lord.
He has scattered the proud and exalted the humble,
guided His children lest they stumble:
My spirit rejoices in God my Saviour.

Mothers' Song
CHORAL/SOLO (*spoken*).
    Mothers
    Mothers of Africa
    Mothers of Asia
    Mothers of all suffering humankind
    Pray for us.
    Mothers
    Mothers of all murdered children
    Mothers of all plague victims
    Mothers of the starving
    Say with us
    These thoughts of our dear dead
    Fruits of our bodies
    Torn from the branch
    Will always stay with us.
    Mothers
    Mothers of all nations
    Mothers at the stations
    of the cross.
    Cry with us at our loss.

(*Sung.*)
(*Verse One*)
    Mothers
    Who must suffer while men fight
    Mothers
    Waiting through the anxious night
    Mothers
    Who endure their starving eyes
    Mothers
    Who must hear their dying cries
    Mothers

(*Verse Two*)
    Mothers
    Who must bear the fruits of war
    Mothers
    Who have known it all before

Mothers
Who are waiting in the rain
Mothers
Dry your tears and start again

(*Spoken*.)

Mothers
Mothers of dead children everywhere lament
And curse the tyrant's hand
The blood of these poor innocents
Cries out throughout the land
To be remembered.

(*Sung*.)

Mothers
Who must bear the fruits of war
Mothers
Who have known it all before
Mothers
Who are waiting in the rain
Mothers
Dry your tears and start again.

Father, Father II (Olivet)

BOY'S VOICE.

Father, Father
Why have You forsaken me?
Please don't leave me
Here among my enemies
One touch of Your hand
And You could set me free
Father, Father
Why have You forsaken me?

Father, Father
Why have You forsaken me?
Please don't leave me
In despair and misery
If You love Your Son
Then come and comfort me
Father, Father
Why have You forsaken me?

Father, Father III (Crucifixion)

BOY'S VOICE.

Father, Father
Why have You forsaken me?
Please don't leave me
Dying on this awful tree
One touch of Your hand
Could take this pain from me
Father, Father
Why have You forsaken me?

Father, Father
Why have You forsaken me?
Please don't leave me
Hanging here in agony
If You love Your Son
Then come and rescue me
Father, Father
Why have You forsaken me?

Stabat Mater

CHORUS.
> *Stabat Mater dolorosa*
> *Juxta crucem lacrimosa,*
> *Dum pendebat Filius.*

MARY.
> How much grief can a woman bear?
> How much pain can a mother share
> with her own son hanging there?
>
> How can she bear the awful loss?
> How can she contemplate the cross
> where He dies in agony?
>
> How can I stand by and see
> My only Son depart from me
> Fastened to this dreadful tree?
>
> And why the fearful sacrifice
> He must make to pay the price
> That saves us all from sin?
> Let it begin.

(*Spoken.*)
> He will be crowned in Heaven.
> King of all but Him who made Him in me.
> Soon He will be free.

(*Sung.*)
> Lord, let the next one be me.

CHORUS.
> *Stabat Mater dolorosa,*
> *Juxta crucem lacrimosa,*
> *Dum pendebat Filius.*
>
> Amen.

Joy and Resurrection

CHORUS.
> Joy and resurrection
> End to mortal strife
> A triumph over Evil
> Bringing everlasting life.

MARY.
> Here is the crown of His passion
> Here is the flower of His pain
> Now is an end to sorrow
> Only my love remains.

PETER.
> Now He ascends to Heaven
> To sit by His Father's side
> All who believe will follow
> Sinners renounce their pride.

CHORUS.
> Joy and resurrection
> End to mortal strife
> A triumph over Evil
> Bringing everlasting life.

QUARTET.
> Heaven's gate waits before us
> So do the depths of Hell
> What kind of fate awaits you?
> Only you alone can tell.

CHORUS.
> Joy and resurrection
> End to mortal strife
> A triumph over Evil
> Bringing everlasting life.